CONQUERING THE FEAR OF FAILURE

Dr. Maxwell Shimba

Shimba Publishing LLC
Printed in the United States of America

First Printing Edition, 2024

Table of Contents

PREFACE

Conquering the Fear of Failure

Conquering the fear of failure is the empowering process of overcoming the paralyzing and often irrational dread of not meeting expectations or achieving desired outcomes. It involves dismantling the psychological barriers that inhibit progress, growth, and success by reshaping one's mindset, adopting effective strategies, and developing a resilient approach to challenges. Conquering this fear involves recognizing its presence, understanding its origins and impact, and then implementing actionable steps to transform it into a driving force for personal development and achievement.

At its core, the fear of failure is an emotional response rooted in the anticipation of negative consequences. It emerges when individuals attach their self-worth and identity to their successes, causing them to perceive failure as a reflection of their abilities and value. This fear can manifest as avoidance of risks, procrastination, or a reluctance to pursue ambitious goals. Left unaddressed, it can limit potential, hinder growth, and lead to missed opportunities.

Conquering the fear of failure requires a multi-faceted approach:

1. Mindset Shift: Central to conquering this fear is reshaping one's mindset. Embracing a growth mindset involves recognizing that failures are not definitive verdicts on competence, but rather stepping stones toward improvement. It's about understanding that setbacks are part of the journey and provide valuable lessons for growth.

2. Self-Compassion: Treating oneself with kindness and understanding, especially in the face of failure, fosters emotional resilience. Self-compassion acknowledges that everyone makes mistakes and faces challenges, promoting a balanced and forgiving view of oneself.

3. Realistic Goal Setting: Establishing achievable goals and breaking them down into manageable steps reduces the overwhelming pressure often associated with the fear of failure. Celebrating small wins along the way reinforces a sense of progress and accomplishment.

4. Embracing Failure as Feedback: Viewing failure as valuable feedback rather than a personal defeat reframes its significance.

Analyzing failures objectively can provide insights into areas for improvement and guide future actions.

5. Taking Calculated Risks: Learning to embrace calculated risks is pivotal in conquering the fear of failure. Understanding that risks are inherent in the pursuit of growth and success encourages a proactive and adventurous approach to challenges.

6. Building Resilience: Developing emotional and psychological resilience equips individuals to navigate setbacks and bounce back stronger. Resilience involves cultivating coping strategies, emotional regulation, and a positive outlook in the face of adversity.

7. Mindfulness and Acceptance: Practicing mindfulness cultivates present-moment awareness, helping individuals detach from anxious thoughts about potential failures. Acceptance of both successes and failures fosters a sense of inner peace and reduces fear-driven reactions.

8. Supportive Network: Surrounding oneself with a supportive network of friends, mentors, and peers provides encouragement and perspective, reminding individuals that they are not alone in their journey.

Conquering the fear of failure is an ongoing process, marked by self-discovery, growth, and the cultivation of inner strength. It is a journey of transformation that empowers individuals to step outside their comfort zones, embrace challenges, and ultimately reach their full potential. Through the integration of these strategies, one can liberate themselves from the chains of fear and embark on a path of self-empowerment, achievement, and a more fulfilling life, in contrast, from a psychological perspective, it involves understanding the intricate workings of the human mind, emotions, and behavior in order to overcome the paralyzing effects of this fear. It entails a multifaceted approach that encompasses cognitive, emotional, and behavioral dimensions, all of which interact to shape our responses to failure-related stimuli. Let's delve into the psychological view of conquering the fear of failure:

1. Cognitive Restructuring: At the heart of conquering the fear of failure is cognitive restructuring. This involves identifying and challenging negative thought patterns and irrational beliefs associated with failure. Individuals tend to engage in catastrophic thinking, imagining the worst-case scenarios, which intensifies the fear. Cognitive

restructuring aims to replace these distorted thoughts with more rational, balanced, and realistic perspectives. By reframing failure as an opportunity for growth and learning, individuals can transform their mindset and reduce the fear's grip.

2. Self-Efficacy and Mastery: Self-efficacy, a concept introduced by psychologist Albert Bandura, refers to an individual's belief in their ability to execute tasks and achieve goals. Conquering the fear of failure involves building a sense of self-efficacy by setting achievable goals and gradually increasing the complexity of challenges. Successes, even small ones, contribute to a sense of mastery and reinforce the belief that one can effectively handle failures.

3. Exposure Therapy: Exposure therapy, commonly used to treat anxiety disorders, can be applied to conquer the fear of failure. Gradual and controlled exposure to failure-related situations helps individuals confront their fears in a controlled manner. Over time, repeated exposure diminishes the fear's intensity, making it more manageable.

4. Self-Compassion: Psychologist Kristin Neff's concept of self-compassion is crucial in conquering the fear of failure. Self-compassion involves treating oneself with kindness, understanding, and non-judgmental acceptance, especially during times of failure. By cultivating self-compassion, individuals learn to respond to failure with self-soothing and self-support, reducing the fear's emotional impact.

5. Emotional Regulation: Emotions play a significant role in the fear of failure. Learning to regulate emotions effectively helps individuals manage the anxiety, shame, and self-doubt associated with failure. Techniques such as mindfulness meditation and deep breathing can enhance emotional regulation, allowing individuals to approach failure with a calmer and more composed mindset.

6. Positive Reinforcement: Positive reinforcement involves rewarding desired behaviors to increase their occurrence. In the context of conquering the fear of failure, individuals can reward themselves for facing challenges and taking risks, irrespective of the outcome. This helps shift the focus from a results-oriented perspective to valuing the effort and courage displayed.

7. Attribution Theory: Attribution theory explores how individuals attribute causes to their successes and failures. By adopting an internal, controllable attribution for successes and viewing failures as external and temporary, individuals can diminish the fear of failure.

This attributional shift empowers them to take responsibility for their successes and view failures as valuable learning experiences.

8. Cognitive Behavioral Techniques: Cognitive-behavioral techniques involve identifying, challenging, and modifying negative thought patterns and behaviors. By consciously altering maladaptive behaviors associated with the fear of failure, individuals can rewire their cognitive processes and respond more constructively to failure-related situations.

Conquering the fear of failure is not about eradicating failure from one's life, but rather transforming one's relationship with it. It involves cultivating a resilient mindset, adopting adaptive strategies, and developing the emotional and cognitive tools needed to navigate failures with courage, self-compassion, and a growth-oriented perspective. In this psychological journey, individuals gradually disempower the fear of failure, unlocking the door to personal growth, achievement, and a more fulfilling life, in contrast, from a biblical perspective, it draws wisdom and guidance from the teachings of the Bible to address this universal human struggle. The Bible offers profound insights and principles that can empower individuals to overcome the paralyzing grip of fear and embrace a path of faith, courage, and growth. Here is the biblical view on conquering the fear of failure:

1. Trusting in God's Sovereignty: The Bible reminds us of God's sovereignty over our lives and circumstances. Proverbs 3:5-6 encourages us to trust in the Lord with all our hearts and lean not on our own understanding. This trust in God's plan and providence can alleviate the fear of failure, knowing that God's purposes prevail even in the face of setbacks.

2. Embracing God's Grace: The biblical concept of grace assures us that our worth and identity are not determined by our achievements or failures. Ephesians 2:8-9 teaches that we are saved by grace through faith, not by our works. Embracing this truth allows us to let go of the fear of failure rooted in seeking validation through success.

3. Overcoming Fear with Faith: The Bible repeatedly encourages us to replace fear with faith. Joshua 1:9 reminds us to be strong and courageous, not to be afraid or discouraged, for the Lord is with us wherever we go. Faith enables us to confront challenges and failures with confidence, trusting that God's strength sustains us.

4. Learning from Failure: The Bible portrays numerous figures who faced failures and yet learned and grew from them. The apostle Peter, for example, denied Jesus three times but later became a pillar of faith. Romans 8:28 assures us that God works all things for the good of those who love Him, including our failures.

5. Persevering Through Trials: Biblical stories exemplify perseverance through trials and failures. James 1:2-4 encourages us to consider it pure joy when we face trials, knowing that they produce perseverance and character. Viewing failures as opportunities for growth aligns with the biblical principle of enduring challenges.

6. Renewing the Mind: The Bible emphasizes the renewal of our minds to align with God's truth. Romans 12:2 encourages transformation by the renewing of our minds. Conquering the fear of failure involves replacing negative thought patterns with God's promises, cultivating a mindset grounded in faith rather than fear.

7. Finding Strength in Weakness: The Bible teaches that God's power is made perfect in our weaknesses. 2 Corinthians 12:9-10 reveals that God's grace is sufficient, even in our weaknesses and failures. Embracing our limitations allows us to rely on God's strength and experience His transformative work.

8. Seeking Wisdom: The fear of failure can be diminished through seeking godly wisdom. Proverbs 3:13-18 extols the value of wisdom, which helps us navigate challenges and make informed decisions. Seeking God's wisdom enables us to approach potential failures with discernment and understanding.

In the biblical view, conquering the fear of failure involves an alignment of our hearts, minds, and actions with God's truth and promises. It calls for trust in God's plan, reliance on His grace, and a willingness to learn, persevere, and grow through challenges. By embracing a faith-centered perspective, individuals can transcend the fear of failure and embrace a journey of spiritual and personal development, anchored in God's love and guidance.

In life, we often encounter challenges that push us outside our comfort zones. One of the most common barriers to personal growth and success is the fear of failure. This paralyzing fear can prevent us from pursuing our dreams, taking risks, and ultimately living a fulfilling life. However, with the right mindset and strategies, it is possible to overcome this fear and embrace success. In this book, we will explore practical techniques and actionable steps to help you conquer the fear of failure and unlock your true potential.

Life is a journey filled with twists and turns, where challenges often beckon us to venture beyond the confines of our comfort zones. Yet, amidst these opportunities for growth and transformation, there stands a formidable obstacle—the fear of failure. This pervasive fear, like a shadow, has the power to cast doubt on our ambitions, hinder our progress, and shackle us from realizing our true potential.

The fear of failure is a deeply ingrained emotion that finds its roots in the vulnerability of the unknown. It whispers doubt into our ears, causing us to question our abilities and the possibility of success. It thrives on the anticipation of negative outcomes, conjuring images of disappointment, humiliation, and shattered dreams. This paralyzing fear becomes a self-imposed barrier that obstructs our path, preventing us from pursuing our passions, seizing opportunities, and embracing the fullness of life.

However, within the depths of this fear lies the potential for transformation. Just as a seedling must break through its shell to grow, we too must confront and conquer the fear of failure to unlock our true potential. The journey from fear to success is not linear, but it is a path laden with tools and strategies that empower us to transcend our limitations.

In the pages of this book, we embark on an exploration of the human psyche, delving into the intricate workings of the fear of failure and its impact on our lives. Through a combination of scientific insights, psychological understanding, and practical wisdom, we will unravel the threads that bind us to this fear and discover how to break free.

I will illuminate the power of mindset—the cornerstone of our approach. With the right mindset, the fear of failure transforms from a paralyzing force into a catalyst for growth. Through deliberate shifts in perspective, we can reframe failure as a stepping stone, a teacher that guides us toward our goals rather than an obstacle that hinders us.

But understanding alone is not enough; action is the key that unlocks transformation. This book is a guide, a roadmap that outlines actionable steps and practical techniques. From cultivating resilience to embracing vulnerability, from setting achievable goals to practicing self-compassion, we will navigate a landscape of strategies designed to dismantle the fear of failure brick by brick.

Embedded within these pages are stories of individuals who have traversed their own fear-ridden journeys and emerged stronger, wiser, and more triumphant. Their experiences serve as beacons of hope, demonstrating that the fear of failure, while formidable, can be conquered.

As you embark on this journey of self-discovery and empowerment, remember that you are not alone. This book is a companion, a source of guidance and encouragement. It invites you to engage, reflect, and apply the principles unveiled within its chapters to your own life.

Ultimately, the message is clear: The fear of failure is not an insurmountable wall, but a challenge to be embraced. With an open heart and a willingness to learn, you can transcend this fear and embark on a path of growth, success, and fulfillment. The journey awaits, and within its twists and turns lies the potential to unlock the doors to your true potential.

DR. MAXWELL SHIMBA

CHAPTER ONE
UNDERSTANDING THE FEAR
OF FAILURE

Understanding the Fear of Failure

The fear of failure is a complex and deeply ingrained psychological phenomenon that can significantly impact our lives, often preventing us from pursuing our goals and realizing our full potential. This fear stems from a combination of evolutionary, societal, and personal factors, and its effects can be far-reaching, affecting our thoughts, emotions, and behaviors.

At its core, the fear of failure can be traced back to our evolutionary history. In primitive times, failure had more immediate and dire consequences, such as endangering one's survival or the survival of the group. This instinctual fear served as a protective mechanism, ensuring that individuals remained cautious and avoided potentially dangerous situations. While modern society has evolved significantly, remnants of this survival-based fear still linger in our psyche, leading us to be wary of failure and its potential repercussions.

Societal influences also play a significant role in the development of the fear of failure. From a young age, we are exposed to societal expectations and norms that define success and failure. These standards create a sense of pressure to meet certain benchmarks, and falling short of these standards can evoke feelings of shame, disappointment, and inadequacy. Additionally, the education system and cultural attitudes toward mistakes can further reinforce the fear of failure, as mistakes are often stigmatized rather than celebrated as opportunities for learning.

On a personal level, our experiences and upbringing shape our attitudes toward success and failure. Early life experiences, such as overly critical parenting or a lack of support, can lead to the internalization of negative beliefs about one's abilities. Perfectionism, a common trait among those who fear failure, can develop as a coping mechanism to avoid potential criticism or rejection. Over time, these beliefs and behaviors become deeply ingrained, influencing our self-esteem, self-worth, and overall self-concept.

The fear of failure manifests in various ways, both cognitively and emotionally. Negative thought patterns, often rooted in self-doubt and self-criticism, can create a cycle of rumination and anxiety. The anticipation of failure can lead to procrastination and avoidance of challenges, limiting our willingness to take risks and explore new opportunities. This avoidance, in turn, reinforces the fear and prevents us from experiencing growth and personal development.

Emotionally, the fear of failure triggers stress responses in the body, including increased heart rate, shallow breathing, and muscle tension. These physical reactions are a manifestation of the body's "fight or flight" response, which is activated in the presence of perceived threats. Over time, chronic stress related to the fear of failure can contribute to mental health issues such as anxiety and depression, further perpetuating the cycle of avoidance and negative thinking.

In essence, the fear of failure is a multifaceted phenomenon that draws from our evolutionary past, societal influences, and personal experiences. Its impact can range from inhibiting our decision-making and risk-taking abilities to causing emotional distress and limiting our potential. However, understanding the origins and mechanisms of this fear is a crucial first step in overcoming it. By recognizing that failure is a natural part of the learning process, challenging negative thought patterns, and gradually exposing ourselves to calculated risks, we can begin to break free from the grip of the fear of failure and unlock our true potential for growth and success.

Understanding the Fear of Failure: A Scientific Exploration

The fear of failure is a complex psychological phenomenon that can impact various aspects of our lives, from pursuing our goals to making important decisions. It is rooted in both evolutionary and cognitive processes and can have significant effects on our emotions, behaviors, and overall well-being. By delving into the scientific reasoning behind the fear of failure, we can gain a deeper understanding of its origins and mechanisms.

Evolutionary Basis:

From an evolutionary perspective, the fear of failure can be traced back to our ancestors' survival instincts. Early humans faced constant threats in their environment, such as predators and scarcity of resources. In this context, failure or making mistakes could have had life-threatening consequences. As a result, the brain evolved to prioritize avoiding potential failures as a means of ensuring survival.

Neurobiological Mechanisms:

1. Amygdala Activation: The amygdala, a part of the brain associated with emotional processing and threat detection, plays a crucial role in the fear of failure. Research using neuroimaging techniques, such as functional magnetic resonance imaging (fMRI), has shown that the amygdala is activated in response to situations that are perceived as potential failures or threats to one's self-esteem.

2. Hypothalamic-Pituitary-Adrenal (HPA) Axis: The fear of failure triggers the body's stress response, leading to the activation of the HPA axis and the release of stress hormones like cortisol. Chronic activation of the stress response due to fear of failure can have negative implications for both mental and physical health.

Cognitive Processes:

1. Perfectionism: Perfectionism is a cognitive trait often associated with the fear of failure. Individuals with high levels of perfectionism set unrealistically high standards for themselves and fear falling short of these standards. Research has linked perfectionism to increased anxiety and lower self-esteem.

2. Negative Self-Evaluation: The fear of failure is often accompanied by negative self-evaluation. Individuals may

catastrophize potential failures, imagining the worst possible outcomes. This cognitive bias can contribute to heightened anxiety and avoidance behaviors.

Psychological Impact:

1. Avoidance Behavior: The fear of failure can lead to avoidance behaviors, where individuals refrain from taking risks or pursuing opportunities to prevent the possibility of failure. This avoidance can limit personal growth, hinder achievement, and perpetuate feelings of stagnation.

2. Low Self-Esteem and Self-Worth: Constant fear of failure can erode self-esteem and self-worth. When failure is seen as a reflection of one's competence or value, individuals may struggle with feelings of inadequacy and self-doubt.

Overcoming the Fear of Failure:

Scientific understanding of the fear of failure provides insights into strategies for overcoming it:

1. Cognitive Restructuring: Cognitive-behavioral techniques can help individuals reframe their thoughts about failure. By challenging irrational beliefs and replacing negative self-talk with more realistic and positive perspectives, individuals can reduce the fear of failure.

2. Exposure Therapy: Gradual exposure to situations associated with the fear of failure can help desensitize individuals to the anxiety-provoking stimuli. Over time, repeated exposure can lead to decreased fear responses.

3. Mindfulness and Acceptance: Mindfulness practices can help individuals observe their fear of failure without judgment and cultivate a non-reactive stance. This can reduce the emotional intensity of the fear and promote a sense of acceptance.

4. Positive Self-Affirmations: Engaging in positive self-affirmations and self-compassion exercises can counteract the negative self-evaluation associated with the fear of failure, promoting a more balanced and self-supportive mindset.

Accordingly, the fear of failure is a multifaceted phenomenon with deep-rooted evolutionary and cognitive underpinnings. Understanding its neurobiological mechanisms and psychological impact empowers individuals to address and overcome this fear. By utilizing evidence-based strategies and interventions, individuals can reshape their relationship with failure, cultivate resilience, and pursue their goals with greater confidence and determination. As science continues to unravel the intricacies of human behavior, the journey toward mastering the fear of failure becomes a promising path toward personal growth and well-being.

Biblical view:

The fear of failure is a deeply rooted emotional response that can hinder personal growth and progress. This fear often stems from a sense of inadequacy, self-doubt, and the anticipation of negative outcomes. In the Bible, various passages offer insights into understanding and overcoming the fear of failure, providing guidance and encouragement to navigate this common human struggle.

One of the key verses that addresses the fear of failure is found in Joshua 1:9 (NIV): "Have I not commanded you? Be strong and courageous. Do not be afraid; do not be discouraged, for the Lord your God will be with you wherever you go." This verse reminds us that God's presence and support are always with us, even in the face of challenges and potential failures. It encourages us to be courageous and resolute, knowing that divine guidance is a constant source of strength.

The fear of failure often arises from a fixed mindset, where we believe our abilities and worth are static. However, Philippians 4:13 (NIV) reassures us: "I can do all this through him who gives me strength." This verse emphasizes that our strength and capabilities come from God, enabling us to overcome obstacles and achieve what may seem impossible. It encourages us to shift from a fixed mindset to a growth mindset, trusting in God's empowerment.

In Psalm 73:26 (NIV), we read, "My flesh and my heart may fail, but God is the strength of my heart and my portion forever." This verse reminds us that human frailty is a natural part of our existence, but God's strength is unwavering. It teaches us that even in the face of failure, God remains our source of strength and sustenance. This perspective can help alleviate the fear of failure, knowing that God's provision is everlasting.

Romans 8:28 (NIV) offers solace in times of perceived failure: "And we know that in all things God works for the good of those who love him, who have been called according to his purpose." This verse assures us that God can use our failures and setbacks for a greater purpose. It encourages us to trust in God's divine plan and see failures as stepping stones toward growth and spiritual development.

Ultimately, 2 Timothy 1:7 (NIV) provides a powerful reminder: "For the Spirit God gave us does not make us timid, but gives us power, love and self-discipline." This verse reinforces that fear is not from God but rather from our own insecurities. It empowers us to embrace God's Spirit within us, which equips us with the courage, love, and self-discipline needed to overcome the fear of failure.

In summary, the fear of failure is a common human struggle, but it can be addressed with the guidance and wisdom found in the Bible. Through verses like Joshua 1:9, Philippians 4:13, Psalm 73:26, Romans 8:28, and 2 Timothy 1:7, we are reminded of God's presence, strength, and purpose in our lives. These verses encourage us to shift our mindset, trust in God's plan, and rely on His empowering Spirit to conquer the fear of failure and embark on a journey of growth and transformation.

1.1 The origins and impact of the fear of failure

The fear of failure is a deeply ingrained emotional response that finds its origins in a complex interplay of evolutionary, societal, and personal factors. This fear can have profound effects on our thoughts, emotions, behaviors, and overall well-being.

From an evolutionary perspective, the fear of failure can be traced back to our ancestors' survival instincts. In primitive times, failure often meant a genuine threat to one's survival – a failed hunt or a lack of resources could lead to dire consequences. As a result, an inherent fear of failure developed as a mechanism to protect individuals and ensure their continued existence. While modern society has evolved, remnants of this survival-based fear still influence our psyche, causing us to view failure as a potential threat to our well-being.

Societal influences play a significant role in shaping our fear of failure. From a young age, we are exposed to societal expectations, standards of success, and a prevailing emphasis on achievements. The pressure to meet these standards can create a sense of inadequacy and fear of falling short. Educational systems often emphasize grades and performance, reinforcing the idea that failure is unacceptable. Additionally, cultural attitudes toward mistakes can amplify the fear, as they may be seen as signs of weakness rather than opportunities for growth.

On a personal level, early life experiences and upbringing contribute to the development of the fear of failure. Childhood experiences of criticism, rejection, or being punished for mistakes can lead to internalized beliefs that failure is unacceptable and shameful. Perfectionism, a common trait among those who fear failure, may develop as a coping mechanism to avoid potential criticism or disappointment. Over time, these beliefs become deeply ingrained, impacting self-esteem and self-worth.

The impact of the fear of failure is far-reaching. Cognitively, it can lead to negative thought patterns such as self-doubt, rumination, and catastrophic thinking. These thought patterns intensify anxiety and undermine self-confidence, creating a self-fulfilling prophecy where the fear of failure becomes a barrier to success. Emotionally, the fear of failure triggers stress responses, releasing hormones like cortisol that contribute to feelings of anxiety and unease. Chronic stress related to this fear can lead to mental health issues such as depression and burnout.

Behaviorally, the fear of failure can result in avoidance behaviors and procrastination. Individuals may shy away from taking risks, pursuing opportunities, or setting ambitious goals to prevent the possibility of failure. This avoidance hinders personal and professional growth and limits the potential for innovation and creativity.

In relationships, the fear of failure can strain social interactions. The fear of being judged or rejected due to perceived failures can lead to withdrawal and isolation, preventing individuals from forming meaningful connections.

Accordingly, the fear of failure has multifaceted origins rooted in evolution, societal influences, and personal experiences. This fear, while once a survival mechanism, now hinders our growth, potential, and well-being. Its impact is evident in negative thought patterns, emotional distress, avoidance behaviors, and strained relationships. Acknowledging the origins and understanding the impact of this fear is crucial to overcoming it and unlocking our true potential for growth and success. Through self-awareness, mindset shifts, and gradual exposure to challenges, we can navigate the fear of failure and embrace a more empowered and fulfilling life.

The Origins and Impact of the Fear of Failure: A Psychological Exploration.

The fear of failure is a pervasive and deeply rooted psychological phenomenon that can profoundly impact various aspects of an individual's thoughts, emotions, behaviors, and overall well-being. Rooted in early experiences, cognitive processes, and socio-cultural influences, the fear of failure can shape one's self-perception, decision-making, and pursuit of goals. By delving into the psychological explanation of its origins and impact, we can gain a comprehensive understanding of this intricate and often limiting fear.

Origins of the Fear of Failure:

1. Early Experiences and Conditioning: The fear of failure can trace its origins to early childhood experiences, including how parents, caregivers, or authority figures responded to mistakes or setbacks. If an individual experienced criticism, harsh punishment, or an emphasis on achievement at an early age, it could lead to a fear of failure as they associate it with negative outcomes.

2. Social Comparison and Expectations: Societal and cultural influences play a role in shaping an individual's fear of failure. Living in a competitive and achievement-oriented culture can foster a constant need to compare oneself with others and meet external expectations, leading to heightened fear of falling short.

3. Cognitive Processes:

a. Perceived Self-Worth: An individual's self-worth can become closely intertwined with their achievements and successes. The fear of failure emerges when they perceive that a failure threatens their sense of self-worth and identity.

b. Catastrophic Thinking: Cognitive biases, such as catastrophizing, amplify the fear of failure. Individuals tend to exaggerate the potential negative consequences of failure, leading to heightened anxiety and avoidance behaviors.

Impact of the Fear of Failure:

1. Performance Anxiety: The fear of failure can lead to performance anxiety, causing individuals to feel tense, overwhelmed, or even immobilized when faced with tasks or situations where they fear falling short of expectations.

2. Procrastination and Avoidance: Fear of failure often results in procrastination or avoidance of tasks that carry a perceived risk of failure. This avoidance behavior can hinder progress, delay achievement, and contribute to a cycle of increased anxiety.

3. Low Self-Esteem and Self-Efficacy: Chronic fear of failure can erode self-esteem and self-efficacy—the belief in one's ability to achieve goals. This negative self-view reinforces the fear and creates a self-fulfilling prophecy.

4. Impaired Decision-Making: Fear of failure can influence decision-making, causing individuals to make choices based on avoiding failure rather than pursuing opportunities aligned with their values and goals.

5. Stagnation and Missed Opportunities: The fear of failure can hinder personal growth and development. Individuals may avoid

challenges or new experiences, resulting in a stagnant comfort zone and missed opportunities for learning and advancement.

Overcoming the Fear of Failure:

1. Self-Compassion: Practicing self-compassion involves treating oneself with kindness and understanding, even in the face of failure. This shifts the focus from self-criticism to self-care and promotes emotional resilience.

2. Cognitive Restructuring: Identifying and challenging negative thought patterns and cognitive distortions associated with failure can help reframe perceptions and reduce anxiety.

3. Exposure Therapy: Gradual exposure to feared situations can desensitize individuals to the fear of failure, leading to decreased anxiety over time.

4. Goal Setting and Achievement: Setting realistic goals, breaking them into manageable steps, and celebrating small wins along the way can build a sense of accomplishment and counteract the fear of failure.

5. Mindfulness and Acceptance: Mindfulness practices cultivate present-moment awareness and acceptance of thoughts and feelings, reducing the emotional intensity of the fear of failure.

Conclusion:

The fear of failure is a complex psychological construct shaped by early experiences, cognitive processes, and socio-cultural influences. Its impact extends to performance, decision-making, self-esteem, and personal growth. Recognizing the origins and understanding the psychological mechanisms behind the fear of failure empowers individuals to address and overcome it. Through self-compassion, cognitive restructuring, exposure therapy, goal setting, and mindfulness, individuals can reshape their relationship with failure, embrace challenges, and pursue their goals with renewed confidence and resilience. As we navigate the intricate landscape of human psychology, the journey toward conquering the fear of failure becomes a transformative path toward self-discovery, growth, and fulfillment.

The fear of failure, a common human struggle, is rooted in a combination of evolutionary history, societal pressures, and personal experiences. This fear can have profound effects on our thoughts, emotions, behaviors, and spiritual well-being. Through the lens of the Bible, we can gain insights into both the origins and impact of this fear.

Origins of Fear of Failure: From an evolutionary perspective, the fear of failure can be understood as a vestige of humanity's survival instincts. In Genesis 3:10 (NIV), Adam expressed fear and shame after sinning: "I heard you in the garden, and I was afraid because I was naked; So, I hid." This fear of vulnerability and exposure mirrors the instinctual fear of failure, which historically signaled danger and threatened survival. Though the world has changed, remnants of this primal fear continue to influence our thoughts and actions.

Societal influences also contribute to the fear of failure. Proverbs 29:25 (NIV) cautions: "Fear of man will prove to be a snare, but whoever trusts in the Lord is kept safe." The pressure to conform to societal expectations and standards can trap us in a cycle of fearing the opinions of others. These external pressures often magnify the fear of failure, making us hesitant to pursue our dreams due to the potential for judgment or rejection.

Impact of Fear of Failure: Cognitively, the fear of failure can lead to negative thought patterns and self-doubt. Psalm 42:11 (NIV) captures this internal struggle: "Why, my soul, are you downcast? Why so disturbed within me?" This psalm reflects the mental distress caused by fear and doubt. Negative thoughts can breed anxiety and hinder our ability to see ourselves as God sees us – fearfully and wonderfully made (Psalm 139:14).

Emotionally, the fear of failure can manifest as stress and anxiety. In Philippians 4:6-7 (NIV), we are encouraged: "Do not be anxious about anything, but in every situation, by prayer and petition, with thanksgiving, present your requests to God. And the peace of God, which transcends all understanding, will guard your hearts and your minds in Christ Jesus." God's peace can replace the anxiety brought on by fear of failure, offering solace and assurance.

Behaviorally, the fear of failure can lead to avoidance and procrastination. In the parable of the talents (Matthew 25:14-30), the servant who buried his talent out of fear represents those who shy away from taking risks. This parable illustrates that burying our talents – avoiding challenges and opportunities – results in spiritual stagnation and missed blessings.

Spiritually, the fear of failure can impede our relationship with God. In Isaiah 41:10 (NIV), God promises: "So do not fear, for I am with you; do not be dismayed, for I am your God. I will strengthen you and help you; I will uphold you with my righteous right hand." Fear can hinder our trust in God's plans and provision, limiting our spiritual growth and intimacy with Him.

In conclusion, the fear of failure finds its origins in evolutionary survival instincts, societal pressures, and personal experiences. This fear's impact spans cognitive, emotional, behavioral, and spiritual realms. Yet, the Bible offers timeless wisdom, assuring us of God's presence, provision, and peace amid our fears. By leaning on biblical truths, cultivating trust in God, and stepping forward in faith, we can confront the fear of failure and live out our God-given potential.

1.2 Recognizing the signs and symptoms

Recognizing the signs and symptoms of the fear of failure is crucial for addressing and overcoming this paralyzing emotion. Whether it manifests subtly or prominently, the fear of failure can impact various aspects of our lives, hindering personal growth, stifling creativity, and impeding our pursuit of success. By understanding and identifying these signs, we can take proactive steps toward breaking free from its grip.

Cognitively, the fear of failure often generates a pattern of negative thinking. Self-doubt, persistent worry about potential outcomes, and a constant focus on potential mistakes can dominate our thoughts. We may find ourselves excessively ruminating on past failures or catastrophizing future scenarios. These cognitive patterns can lead to a skewed perception of reality, causing us to underestimate our abilities and the potential for positive outcomes.

Emotionally, the fear of failure can trigger a range of intense feelings. Anxiety and restlessness are common emotional responses, often accompanied by a heightened sense of unease or tension. Feelings of inadequacy, shame, and self-criticism may surface, contributing to a diminished sense of self-worth. Over time, these emotional responses can lead to emotional exhaustion, burnout, and even symptoms of depression.

Behaviorally, the fear of failure can lead to avoidance behaviors. We may shy away from taking on new challenges, pursuing opportunities, or setting ambitious goals. This avoidance stems from a desire to sidestep potential failure and the associated negative feelings. Procrastination is another common behavioral sign, as the fear of failure can create a mental block that prevents us from initiating or completing tasks.

Interpersonally, the fear of failure can impact relationships. We might isolate ourselves from others, fearing judgment or rejection if our perceived failures are exposed. This isolation can lead to a sense of loneliness and disconnect. Additionally, the fear of failure can manifest as a reluctance to seek help or collaborate with others, as we may fear appearing incapable or inadequate in front of others.

Physiologically, the fear of failure can trigger stress responses in the body. Increased heart rate, shallow breathing, muscle tension, and even digestive issues can arise as a result of prolonged stress. These physical symptoms can contribute to a cycle of heightened anxiety and discomfort, further reinforcing the fear of failure.

Spiritually, the fear of failure can hinder our sense of purpose and alignment with our faith. Doubt in our abilities can translate to doubt in God's plan for us. We may question whether we are living up to our potential or following the path that God intended for us. This can create a spiritual disconnect and rob us of the peace and fulfillment that come from trusting in a higher purpose.

In summary, recognizing the signs and symptoms of the fear of failure is essential for our personal growth and well-being. From negative thought patterns and emotional distress to avoidance behaviors and physical symptoms, these indicators offer valuable insight into the extent to which this fear is affecting our lives. By acknowledging these signs, we can begin the journey toward overcoming the fear of failure through self-awareness, self-compassion, and targeted strategies for growth and transformation.

Recognizing the signs and symptoms of the fear of failure is a crucial step toward understanding and addressing this common human struggle. The Bible offers valuable insights that can help us identify these signs and guide us toward overcoming the paralyzing effects of this fear.

Cognitively, the fear of failure often manifests as negative and self-critical thinking. In Proverbs 12:25 (NIV), we are reminded that "anxiety weighs down the heart, but a kind word cheers it up." When our thoughts are dominated by self-doubt and worry about potential failure, our hearts become burdened. This verse highlights the emotional toll of negative cognitive patterns and the need for uplifting and supportive self-talk.

Emotionally, the fear of failure can lead to feelings of inadequacy and shame. Romans 8:1 (NIV) offers reassurance: "Therefore, there is now no condemnation for those who are in Christ Jesus." This verse reminds us that we are not defined by our failures; rather, we find redemption and freedom in our faith. Embracing this truth can help alleviate the emotional distress caused by the fear of failure.

Behaviorally, the fear of failure often results in avoidance and procrastination. In Matthew 25:24-25 (NIV), the parable of the talents illustrates the consequences of fear-driven inaction: "Then the man who had received one bag of gold came. 'Master,' he said, 'I knew that you are a hard man, harvesting where you have not sown and gathering where you have not scattered seed. So, I was afraid and went out and hid your gold in the ground.'" This servant's fear led to a missed opportunity and unfulfilled potential. Similarly, our avoidance behaviors can hinder our ability to utilize the gifts and talents God has bestowed upon us.

Interpersonally, the fear of failure can strain relationships. In Galatians 6:2 (NIV), we are encouraged to "carry each other's burdens, and in this way, you will fulfill the law of Christ." The fear of being judged or rejected can prevent us from seeking support and sharing our struggles with others. Yet, this verse emphasizes the importance of community and mutual support in times of difficulty.

Physiologically, the fear of failure triggers stress responses. In Psalm 139:14 (NIV), we are reminded of God's intricate design: "I praise you because I am fearfully and wonderfully made; your works are wonderful, I know that full well." Recognizing the fear of failure's impact on our physical well-being reminds us of the importance of caring for our bodies, which are fearfully and wonderfully crafted by God.

Spiritually, the fear of failure can create a rift between us and God's plan for our lives. Jeremiah 29:11 (NIV) reassures us of God's intentions: "For I know the plans I have for you, declares the Lord, plans to prosper you and not to harm you, plans to give you hope and a future." Allowing fear to dictate our actions can hinder us from aligning with God's divine purpose and experiencing the hope and fulfillment He promises.

In conclusion, recognizing the signs and symptoms of the fear of failure is vital for personal growth and spiritual well-being. Through negative cognitive patterns, emotional distress, avoidance behaviors, strained relationships, physical symptoms, and spiritual disconnect, this fear can significantly impact our lives. By anchoring ourselves in biblical truths, such as God's love, forgiveness, and purpose for us, we can overcome the fear of failure and embark on a journey of courage, resilience, and faith.

1.3 Debunking common misconceptions about failure

Failure is a natural and inevitable part of the human experience, yet it often carries a heavy burden of negative connotations and misconceptions. Debunking these misconceptions about failure is essential for cultivating a healthier mindset, embracing personal growth, and unlocking our true potential.

Misconception 1: Failure is a Final Outcome One common misconception about failure is that it signifies a definitive and irreversible endpoint. In reality, failure is often a temporary setback or a stepping stone toward success. Just as in nature, where new growth often emerges from the ashes of what has fallen, failure can lead to valuable insights, learning, and eventual triumph. Failure is a dynamic process, offering opportunities for redirection and improvement.

Misconception 2: Failure Reflects Inadequacy Many people equate failure with personal inadequacy or unworthiness. However, failure is not a reflection of one's identity or worth as an individual. Romans 3:23 (NIV) reminds us, "for all have sinned and fall short of the glory of God." This verse acknowledges the imperfections of humanity, emphasizing that failure is a shared experience. Understanding that even the most accomplished individuals face failure can help dispel the misconception that it defines our value.

Misconception 3: Failure is Avoidable A prevailing misconception is that success is attained by avoiding failure altogether. Yet, this notion overlooks the reality that innovation, growth, and progress often arise from experimenting and taking calculated risks. Proverbs 24:16 (NIV) reinforces this truth: "for though the righteous fall seven times, they rise again." Embracing failure as part of the journey enables us to bounce back and ultimately achieve greater heights.

Misconception 4: Failure Equates to Shame. Shame is a common emotion associated with failure, perpetuating the belief that failure should be hidden or denied. However, vulnerability researcher Brené Brown emphasizes that shame cannot survive empathy and connection. Galatians 6:2 (NIV) supports this principle: "Carry each other's burdens, and in this way, you will fulfill the law of Christ." Sharing our failures with others fosters a sense of connection and empathy, dismantling the misconception that failure should be concealed.

Misconception 5: Failure Diminishes Opportunities Failure is often viewed as a closed door, limiting future opportunities. In truth, failure can open doors to unexpected avenues and fresh perspectives.

Consider Joseph's story in Genesis 50:20 (NIV): "You intended to harm me, but God intended it for good to accomplish what is now being done, the saving of many lives." Joseph's initial failures led to his eventual role in saving many lives. Similarly, our failures can pave the way for new and transformative paths.

Misconception 6: Failure is an Indicator of Effort The misconception that failure is a direct reflection of effort overlooks the myriad factors that contribute to outcomes. Hard work and dedication are important, but external circumstances and unforeseen variables also play a significant role. Ecclesiastes 9:11 (NIV) acknowledges this truth: "The race is not to the swift or the battle to the strong, nor does food come to the wise or wealth to the brilliant or favor to the learned; but time and chance happen to them all."

In conclusion, debunking common misconceptions about failure is vital for fostering a healthier and more empowered perspective. Failure is not a final outcome, does not define our worth, is not always avoidable, need not be hidden in shame, does not limit opportunities, and is not solely indicative of effort. By embracing failure as a catalyst for growth, learning, and resilience, we can navigate life's challenges with courage, grace, and a renewed sense of purpose.

Debunking common misconceptions about failure. Biblical views

Failure is an inevitable and integral part of the human experience, yet it is often accompanied by a host of misconceptions that can hinder personal growth and development. By debunking these misconceptions, we can foster a healthier and more productive relationship with failure, drawing insights from both life's challenges and the wisdom of the Bible.

Misconception 1: Failure is a Mark of Inadequacy One of the most pervasive misconceptions is that failure is a reflection of one's inadequacy or lack of worth. However, in 2 Corinthians 12:9 (NIV), the apostle Paul declares, "But he said to me, 'My grace is sufficient for you, for my power is made perfect in weakness.'" This verse emphasizes that even in moments of failure or weakness, God's grace is sufficient to sustain us. Failure does not define our value in God's eyes; rather, it presents an opportunity for God's strength to shine through our vulnerabilities.

Misconception 2: Failure is Irreversible Another common misconception is that failure is a final and irreversible outcome. Yet, Isaiah 43:18-19 (NIV) offers a different perspective: "Forget the former things; do not dwell on the past. See, I am doing a new thing! Now it springs up; do you not perceive it?" This passage highlights the potential for new beginnings and fresh opportunities, even in the aftermath of failure. God's ability to bring about renewal and transformation can turn what seems like a dead end into a new path of growth.

Misconception 3: Failure is to be Hidden in Shame. Shame often accompanies failure, leading us to believe that our mistakes should be hidden. However, Romans 8:1 (NIV) reminds us, "Therefore, there is now no condemnation for those who are in Christ Jesus." In the eyes of God, we are forgiven and free from condemnation. This truth encourages us to approach failure with honesty and openness, seeking support and learning from our experiences without the burden of shame.

Misconception 4: Failure Diminishes Opportunities The misconception that failure diminishes future opportunities can hinder our willingness to take risks. Yet, Psalm 37:23-24 (NIV) offers reassurance: "The Lord makes firm the steps of the one who delights in him; though he may stumble, he will not fall, for the Lord upholds him with his hand." This passage highlights God's guidance and support, even in times of stumbling. Embracing failure as a stepping stone can lead to unexpected blessings and avenues for growth.

Misconception 5: Failure Reflects Lack of Effort Attributing failure solely to a lack of effort overlooks the complexities of life's challenges. James 1:2-4 (NIV) provides a different perspective: "Consider it pure joy, my brothers and sisters, whenever you face trials of many kinds, because you know that the testing of your faith produces perseverance. Let perseverance finish its work so that you may be mature and complete, not lacking anything." This passage underscores the idea that trials, including failure, contribute to our spiritual growth and maturity.

Misconception 6: Failure is to be Feared Lastly, fearing failure can paralyze us and prevent us from pursuing our dreams. However, Joshua 1:9 (NIV) offers a powerful antidote: "Have I not commanded you? Be strong and courageous. Do not be afraid; do not be discouraged, for the Lord your God will be with you wherever you go." This verse encourages us to face challenges with strength and courage, knowing that God's presence accompanies us on our journey.

In conclusion, debunking common misconceptions about failure is essential for cultivating a resilient and empowered mindset. Through the wisdom of the Bible, we learn that failure does not define our worth, is not irreversible, need not be hidden in shame, does not diminish opportunities, is not solely indicative of effort, and need not be feared. By embracing failure as a catalyst for growth, relying on God's grace, and approaching challenges with courage, we can navigate life's uncertainties with renewed hope and purpose.

1.4 The correlation between failure and growth.

The correlation between failure and growth is a profound and often overlooked aspect of the human journey. While failure is often viewed with apprehension and disappointment, it can be a powerful catalyst for personal and intellectual development, fostering resilience, adaptability, and a deeper understanding of oneself and the world.

Failure serves as a crucible for growth because it challenges our comfort zones and exposes us to new perspectives. When we step out of our familiar routines and confront the unknown, we open ourselves to the possibility of failure. However, this very process is where growth begins. Just as a seed must break through its shell to germinate and grow, we too must break through the barriers of fear and complacency to reach our full potential.

In the realm of education, failure plays a pivotal role in the learning process. Students who encounter challenges and mistakes have the opportunity to engage in reflective thinking, analyzing what went wrong and how to improve. This aligns with the principle of metacognition, where learners become more aware of their thought processes and develop strategies for effective problem-solving. Failure, in this context, is not an endpoint but a stepping stone toward mastery.

The correlation between failure and growth is underscored by the concept of a growth mindset, as championed by psychologist Carol Dweck. Individuals with a growth mindset view failure as an opportunity for learning and development. They understand that abilities can be developed through dedication and hard work. This mindset encourages a willingness to take risks, embrace challenges, and persevere through setbacks, all of which contribute to personal and intellectual growth.

Spiritual and emotional growth are also intricately tied to failure. In times of adversity, we often turn to our faith or inner strength for guidance and solace. The Bible is replete with stories of individuals who faced failure and emerged stronger and more resilient. Consider the story of Job, who experienced profound loss and suffering but ultimately found spiritual growth and a deeper connection with God.

Furthermore, failure nurtures qualities such as humility and empathy. When we falter, we gain a newfound appreciation for the struggles of others and a sense of humility that reminds us of our humanity. This, in turn, strengthens our capacity for compassion and understanding, fostering deeper and more meaningful connections with those around us.

The correlation between failure and growth is evident in the world of innovation and entrepreneurship. Many groundbreaking inventions and discoveries have emerged from a series of failed attempts. The light bulb, for instance, was the result of countless experiments by Thomas Edison, who famously said, "I have not failed. I've just found 10,000 ways that won't work." Failure can act as a guide, directing us toward the right path through a process of trial and error.

In conclusion, failure and growth are intricately linked in a symbiotic relationship. Failure, far from being a sign of inadequacy, is a conduit for growth and development. It challenges our perspectives, fosters resilience, nurtures humility, and cultivates a growth mindset. By embracing failure as a necessary and valuable part of our journey, we open ourselves to the transformative potential that it holds. Just as a phoenix rises from its ashes, we too can rise stronger and more enlightened through the ashes of failure.

The Correlation Between Failure and Growth: Unveiling the Science Behind Resilience.

The interplay between failure and growth is a captivating phenomenon that has been extensively explored by researchers and psychologists. Far from being adversaries, failure and growth are intrinsically linked in a symbiotic relationship that fuels personal development, resilience, and achievement. Scientific evidence and reasoning highlight how failure acts as a catalyst for growth, reshaping our perceptions, skills, and attitudes in profound ways.

1. Neuroplasticity and Learning:

Scientific research has unveiled the brain's remarkable capacity for change, known as neuroplasticity. When we face challenges and failures, the brain undergoes adaptive changes in response. These changes allow us to acquire new skills, refine existing ones, and develop cognitive flexibility. Failure triggers neural pathways associated with learning, leading to improved problem-solving, creativity, and adaptability.

2. Cognitive Restructuring:

Failure compels us to reevaluate our beliefs, assumptions, and strategies. This process, known as cognitive restructuring, is driven by the brain's innate tendency to seek meaning and coherence. When we confront failure, we engage in introspection and analysis, fostering a deeper understanding of our strengths, weaknesses, and areas for improvement. This cognitive restructuring is a pivotal mechanism that fuels personal growth and development.

3. Resilience and Adaptation:

Failure is a natural crucible for resilience—the ability to bounce back from adversity. The experience of failure activates stress response systems, prompting the release of stress hormones like cortisol. Over time, this exposure to manageable stressors enhances our stress tolerance and resilience. Through repeated exposure to failure, we develop emotional regulation skills and coping mechanisms, allowing us to navigate future challenges with greater equanimity.

4. Embracing the Growth Mindset:

Psychologist Carol Dweck's concept of the growth mindset underscores the transformative power of failure. Individuals with a growth mindset perceive failure as a stepping stone to improvement, rather than a final verdict on their abilities. Studies have shown that those with a growth mindset are more likely to view setbacks as opportunities for learning and personal growth. This mindset shift not only enhances motivation but also fosters a resilient approach to challenges.

5. Mastery and Skill Development:

Failure propels us along the path of mastery—a state of continuous improvement and refinement. Psychologist Anders Ericsson's "10,000-hour rule" suggests that deliberate practice, often involving setbacks and failures, is necessary to achieve expertise in any field. Failure acts as a feedback mechanism, guiding us toward areas that require further practice and refinement. With each failure, we inch closer to mastery, cultivating a deep sense of accomplishment and growth.

6. Overcoming Fear and Expanding Comfort Zones:

Failure challenges us to confront our fears and step outside our comfort zones. The discomfort of failure is often the result of venturing into uncharted territory. However, repeated exposure to failure diminishes the emotional intensity associated with these experiences. As we push boundaries, our comfort zone expands, enabling us to take on progressively greater challenges with confidence.

7. Psychological Resilience:

The process of navigating failure fosters psychological resilience—a dynamic quality that enables individuals to cope with stress, adapt to adversity, and maintain psychological well-being. Resilience encompasses emotional regulation, problem-solving skills, and a positive outlook. Failure, as a stimulus for resilience development, equips us with the tools needed to thrive in the face of uncertainty.

Conclusion:

The correlation between failure and growth is rooted in neuroplasticity, cognitive restructuring, resilience development, and the fostering of a growth mindset. Failure's role as a catalyst for learning, mastery, and resilience underscores its transformative potential. As we embrace failure as a natural and essential part of the human experience, we unlock a pathway to personal development, innovation, and achievement. The scientific evidence illuminates the dynamic synergy between failure and growth—a partnership that shapes the trajectory of our lives and empowers us to thrive in a world filled with challenges and opportunities.

The correlation between failure and growth is a profound and meaningful concept that finds resonance in both human experience and the teachings of the Bible. While failure is often perceived negatively, it holds the potential to catalyze remarkable personal and spiritual growth, leading individuals to develop resilience, humility, wisdom, and a deeper connection with their faith.

Scripture is replete with examples that illustrate the transformative power of failure. In Romans 5:3-4 (NIV), the apostle Paul writes, "Not only so, but we also glory in our sufferings, because we know that suffering produces perseverance; perseverance, character; and character, hope." Here, the progression from suffering to hope echoes the correlation between failure and growth. Failure, often accompanied by suffering, can give rise to perseverance – the tenacity to continue despite setbacks. Through this perseverance, character is refined, fostering qualities such as patience, resilience, and humility. Ultimately, this process culminates in the blossoming of hope, demonstrating how growth can emerge from the depths of failure.

The story of Peter, one of Jesus' disciples, exemplifies the transformative potential of failure. In Matthew 26:69-75 (NIV), Peter denies knowing Jesus three times, succumbing to fear and pressure. However, this failure becomes a turning point. After Jesus' resurrection, Peter's encounter with his own weakness leads to profound growth. In

John 21:15-17 (NIV), Jesus reinstates Peter, asking him three times if he loves Him. This mirrors Peter's earlier denials and offers him a chance for redemption. Through this process, Peter's failure becomes a catalyst for growth in his faith and commitment.

Failure can also lead to a deeper understanding of our dependence on God. In 2 Corinthians 12:9-10 (NIV), Paul recounts his experience of seeking relief from a "thorn in the flesh." Instead of removing the thorn, God responds, "My grace is sufficient for you, for my power is made perfect in weakness." Paul's recognition of his weakness and God's sufficiency demonstrates how failure can lead to a humbling awareness of our need for divine strength. This acknowledgment fosters spiritual growth and a closer relationship with God.

The correlation between failure and growth is evident in the realm of personal development. The parable of the talents in Matthew 25:14-30 (NIV) illustrates this concept. Three servants are entrusted with different amounts of talents (currency). While two of them invest and multiply their talents, the third buries his out of fear. Upon the master's return, the first two are commended and entrusted with more, while the third faces consequences for his inaction. This parable illustrates that stepping out in faith, despite the risk of failure, leads to growth and greater opportunities.

Moreover, James 1:2-4 (NIV) highlights the relationship between trials and growth: "Consider it pure joy, my brothers and sisters, whenever you face trials of many kinds, because you know that the testing of your faith produces perseverance. Let perseverance finish its work so that you may be mature and complete, not lacking anything." Trials, including failures, challenge and refine our faith, leading to greater maturity and completeness.

In conclusion, the correlation between failure and growth is a powerful and transformative journey that resonates deeply within both human experiences and biblical teachings. Just as the trials of life can lead to perseverance, character, and hope, failures can be instrumental in shaping our character, deepening our faith, and fostering spiritual growth. Through the stories of Peter, Paul, and the parables shared in the Bible, we are reminded that failure is not an endpoint but a stepping stone toward greater maturity and connection with God. Embracing failure as a catalyst for growth allows us to tap into its hidden potential and emerge stronger, wiser, and more faithful individuals.

CHAPTER TWO
SHIFTING YOUR MINDSET

Shifting Your Mindset

Shifting your mindset involves a deliberate and conscious change in the way you perceive and interpret situations, challenges, and yourself. It is a transformative process that empowers you to adopt a more positive and constructive perspective, enabling you to navigate life's complexities with greater resilience, optimism, and personal growth.

At the core of shifting your mindset is the recognition that your thoughts have a powerful influence on your emotions, behaviors, and overall well-being. The way you interpret events shapes your reactions and decisions. By intentionally altering your thought patterns, you can create a ripple effect that leads to profound changes in your life.

One key aspect of shifting your mindset is cultivating a growth mindset, a concept popularized by psychologist Carol Dweck. A growth mindset embraces the belief that abilities and intelligence can be developed through effort, learning, and persistence. This contrasts with a fixed mindset, which assumes that talents and traits are innate and unchangeable. Embracing a growth mindset allows you to view challenges and failures as opportunities for learning and improvement, rather than as reflections of your inherent worth.

To shift your mindset, it's essential to challenge and reframe negative or limiting beliefs. For instance, if you tend to view failure as a sign of incompetence, you can reframe it as a stepping stone toward success. This shift in perspective allows you to embrace failure as a valuable source of experience and growth.

Mindfulness also plays a significant role in shifting your mindset. Mindfulness involves being present in the moment and observing your thoughts without judgment. Through mindfulness practices, you can become more attuned to your thought patterns and choose to respond to them in a more constructive manner. This heightened awareness empowers you to detach from negative thoughts and replace them with more positive and empowering ones.

Affirmations are another effective tool for shifting your mindset. By repeating positive statements about yourself, your abilities, and your potential, you can gradually reshape your self-perception and boost your confidence. For example, if you often doubt your abilities, you can affirm, "I am capable and resilient. I can overcome challenges and achieve my goals."

Shifting your mindset also involves practicing gratitude. Gratitude helps you focus on the positive aspects of your life and appreciate the blessings you have. It shifts your attention away from what's lacking or negative, fostering a more optimistic outlook. In 1 Thessalonians 5:18 (NIV), we are reminded to "give thanks in all circumstances; for this is God's will for you in Christ Jesus." This biblical principle underscores the transformative power of gratitude in shaping our mindset.

Hence, shifting your mindset is a powerful and intentional process that can lead to profound personal growth and transformation. By embracing a growth mindset, challenging negative beliefs, practicing mindfulness, using affirmations, and cultivating gratitude, you can reshape the way you perceive yourself, challenges, and the world around you. This shift in perspective empowers you to approach life with greater resilience, positivity, and a deep sense of empowerment, enabling you to overcome obstacles and unlock your true potential.

Furthermore, shifting your mindset is a transformative process that involves changing the way you perceive and interpret life's challenges, yourself, and the world around you. It's a conscious effort to adopt a more positive, empowering, and growth-oriented perspective that aligns with your values and goals. This shift has profound implications for your emotional well-being, relationships, and overall quality of life, and it finds resonance in the teachings of the Bible.

1. Embracing a Renewed Mind: In Romans 12:2 (NIV), the apostle Paul encourages believers: "Do not conform to the pattern of this world, but be transformed by the renewing of your mind. Then you will be able to test and approve what God's will is—his good, pleasing and perfect will." This verse highlights the transformative power of renewing your mind. By deliberately shifting your mindset away from worldly patterns and aligning it with God's truth, you can gain clarity on your purpose and navigate life's challenges in accordance with His will.

2. Cultivating a Positive Perspective: Philippians 4:8 (NIV) offers guidance on cultivating a positive and constructive mindset: "Finally, brothers and sisters, whatever is true, whatever is noble, whatever is right, whatever is pure, whatever is lovely, whatever is admirable—if anything is excellent or praiseworthy—think about such things." This verse emphasizes the importance of focusing your thoughts on virtuous and uplifting aspects of life. Shifting your mindset to dwell on positivity and goodness can lead to increased joy and contentment.

3. Overcoming Fear and Doubt: Fear and doubt often hinder personal growth and progress. In 2 Timothy 1:7 (NIV), it is written, "For the Spirit God gave us does not make us timid, but gives us power, love and self-discipline." Shifting your mindset involves tapping into the power and self-discipline that God has provided, enabling you to overcome fear and doubt. By focusing on God's strength within you, you can approach challenges with confidence and courage.

4. Seeing Failure as Growth: James 1:2-4 (NIV) provides insight into the purpose of trials and challenges: "Consider it pure joy, my brothers and sisters, whenever you face trials of many kinds, because you know that the testing of your faith produces perseverance. Let perseverance finish its work so that you may be mature and complete, not lacking anything." This passage highlights the growth that arises from facing trials. Shifting your mindset to view failures and difficulties as opportunities for perseverance and maturity can foster resilience and personal development.

5. Trusting God's Plan: Proverbs 3:5-6 (NIV) guides believers to trust in God's wisdom and guidance: "Trust in the Lord with all your heart and lean not on your own understanding; in all your ways submit to him, and he will make your paths straight." Shifting your mindset involves relinquishing your need for complete control and placing your trust in God's sovereign plan. This shift can alleviate anxiety and empower you to navigate uncertainties with faith and confidence.

In conclusion, shifting your mindset is a transformative journey that aligns with biblical principles and has the potential to enhance your spiritual and emotional well-being. By renewing your mind, cultivating positivity, overcoming fear, embracing growth through challenges, and trusting in God's plan, you can experience a profound shift in your perspective. This shift empowers you to approach life with greater courage, gratitude, and a deep sense of purpose, leading to personal growth and a more fulfilling journey of faith.

2.1 Cultivating a growth mindset

Cultivating a growth mindset is a powerful and transformative approach to life that centers on the belief that abilities, intelligence, and skills can be developed and improved through effort, learning, and perseverance. Coined by psychologist Carol Dweck, the concept of a growth mindset has gained significant traction for its potential to enhance personal and professional development, foster resilience, and unlock untapped potential.

At the heart of a growth mindset is the understanding that challenges and failures are not indicators of fixed limitations, but rather opportunities for growth and learning. Unlike a fixed mindset, which assumes that traits and abilities are innate and unchangeable, a growth mindset embraces the idea that with dedication and hard work, individuals can continuously develop and refine their capabilities.

One key aspect of cultivating a growth mindset is recognizing and reframing the role of effort and setbacks. Instead of viewing effort as a sign of inadequacy or difficulty, individuals with a growth mindset see it as the path to mastery. They understand that progress often requires stepping out of their comfort zones and embracing challenges. Setbacks are seen as stepping stones, providing valuable feedback and insights that guide further improvement.

Another important element of a growth mindset is the willingness to embrace and learn from criticism. Rather than taking criticism personally or defensively, individuals with a growth mindset view it as an opportunity for feedback and growth. They understand that constructive criticism can highlight areas for improvement and lead to better outcomes in the future.

Cultivating a growth mindset also involves fostering a love for learning. Embracing new knowledge and skills is seen as an exciting and enriching experience, rather than a daunting task. This mindset encourages individuals to seek out opportunities for growth, whether through formal education, self-study, or hands-on experiences.

A growth mindset also goes hand in hand with resilience. When faced with setbacks, challenges, or failures, individuals with a growth mindset are more likely to bounce back and persevere. They view obstacles as temporary hurdles that can be overcome with effort and determination. This resilience is grounded in the belief that setbacks are not indicative of unchangeable shortcomings, but rather stepping stones on the path to success.

Incorporating a growth mindset into one's life requires intentional effort and self-awareness. It involves cultivating self-compassion and recognizing that setbacks are a natural part of the learning process. Embracing a growth mindset can also involve seeking out role models and mentors who embody this perspective, as well as surrounding oneself with a supportive community that encourages growth and learning.

Ultimately, cultivating a growth mindset is a journey of personal transformation. By shifting one's perspective from a fixed view of abilities to a belief in the potential for continuous development, individuals can unlock new possibilities, achieve greater resilience, and approach life's challenges with a sense of optimism and empowerment. Whether in education, career, relationships, or personal goals, a growth mindset has the power to unleash untapped potential and pave the way for lasting success.

Cultivating a growth mindset is a transformative journey that aligns with biblical principles and offers profound insights into personal development, resilience, and the pursuit of excellence. Rooted in the belief that abilities and skills can be developed through effort and learning, a growth mindset finds resonance in the teachings of the Bible and empowers individuals to embrace challenges, overcome setbacks, and realize their fullest potential.

1. Embracing Effort and Perseverance: The Bible emphasizes the value of diligence and perseverance in Proverbs 13:4 (NIV): "A sluggard's appetite is never filled, but the desires of the diligent are fully satisfied." This verse underscores the importance of putting in

consistent effort to achieve satisfaction and success. Cultivating a growth mindset aligns with this principle, as it encourages individuals to embrace challenges and setbacks as opportunities for growth rather than reasons for discouragement.

2. Learning from Failure: Failure is a natural part of the growth process, and the Bible offers wisdom on learning from setbacks. In Romans 5:3-4 (NIV), the apostle Paul writes, "We also glory in our sufferings, because we know that suffering produces perseverance; perseverance, character; and character, hope." This progression from suffering to hope reflects the growth mindset's approach to failure. It teaches us that enduring challenges develops resilience, character, and a hopeful outlook.

3. Renewing the Mind: Romans 12:2 (NIV) encourages believers to renew their minds: "Do not conform to the pattern of this world, but be transformed by the renewing of your mind. Then you will be able to test and approve what God's will is—his good, pleasing and perfect will." This verse highlights the transformative power of changing one's perspective. Cultivating a growth mindset involves intentionally shifting from a fixed view of abilities to a belief in the potential for continuous improvement, aligning with the renewal of the mind advocated in this scripture.

4. Embracing Challenges: James 1:2-4 (NIV) offers insight into the value of trials: "Consider it pure joy, my brothers and sisters, whenever you face trials of many kinds, because you know that the testing of your faith produces perseverance. Let perseverance finish its work so that you may be mature and complete, not lacking anything." This passage speaks to the growth that arises from facing challenges with a positive attitude. Cultivating a growth mindset involves viewing challenges as opportunities for spiritual and personal development.

5. Seeking Wisdom and Knowledge: Proverbs 2:6 (NIV) highlights the role of God in granting wisdom: "For the Lord gives wisdom; from his mouth come knowledge and understanding." Cultivating a growth mindset involves a hunger for learning and a willingness to seek knowledge. Just as the pursuit of wisdom is valued in the Bible, individuals with a growth mindset actively seek opportunities to expand their understanding and skills.

6. Being Transformed: The apostle Paul encourages believers to be transformed in Romans 12:2 (NIV): "Do not conform to the pattern of this world, but be transformed by the renewing of your mind." This transformation, rooted in faith and perseverance, mirrors the essence

of a growth mindset. It involves a deliberate shift in thinking that leads to personal and spiritual growth.

In addition, cultivating a growth mindset is a journey that harmonizes with biblical principles and offers valuable insights into personal development, resilience, and the pursuit of excellence. By embracing effort, learning from failure, renewing the mind, embracing challenges, seeking wisdom, and undergoing transformation, individuals can unlock their God-given potential and approach life's challenges with faith, optimism, and a deep sense of purpose.

2.2 Embracing the power of self-belief

Embracing the power of self-belief is a transformative and empowering journey that involves recognizing and harnessing the innate potential within oneself. It is the profound understanding that one's thoughts, attitudes, and beliefs play a pivotal role in shaping actions, outcomes, and overall well-being. By cultivating a strong sense of self-belief, individuals can overcome obstacles, pursue their dreams, and lead more fulfilling lives.

1. Recognizing Inner Potential: At the core of embracing the power of self-belief is the recognition of inherent potential. Psalm 139:14 (NIV) states, "I praise you because I am fearfully and wonderfully made; your works are wonderful, I know that full well." This verse emphasizes the divine creation of each individual and highlights the intrinsic value and uniqueness of every person. Embracing self-belief involves acknowledging this inherent worth and understanding that God has endowed us with the capacity for growth, achievement, and greatness.

2. Overcoming Limiting Beliefs: Self-belief empowers individuals to challenge and overcome limiting beliefs that hinder personal growth. In Mark 9:23 (NIV), Jesus declares, "Everything is possible for one who believes." This statement underscores the transformative power of belief in overcoming seemingly insurmountable challenges. Embracing self-belief involves questioning and dismantling self-imposed limitations, allowing individuals to venture into uncharted territories with confidence and determination.

3. Fostering Resilience: Self-belief is closely intertwined with resilience—the ability to bounce back from adversity. James 1:6 (NIV) advises, "But when you ask, you must believe and not doubt, because the one who doubts is like a wave of the sea, blown and tossed by the wind." This analogy emphasizes the importance of unwavering faith and belief. Embracing self-belief enables individuals to navigate

setbacks and challenges with greater determination, seeing them as opportunities for growth rather than as roadblocks.

4. Pursuing Goals and Dreams: Believing in oneself fuels the pursuit of goals and dreams. Proverbs 16:3 (NIV) states, "Commit to the Lord whatever you do, and he will establish your plans." This verse highlights the synergy between faith, action, and divine support. Embracing self-belief empowers individuals to set ambitious goals, take calculated risks, and persistently work toward their aspirations, trusting that their efforts are aligned with God's plan.

5. Cultivating Positive Mindset: Self-belief nurtures a positive mindset that affects both mental and emotional well-being. Philippians 4:8 (NIV) instructs, "Finally, brothers and sisters, whatever is true, whatever is noble, whatever is right, whatever is pure, whatever is lovely, whatever is admirable—if anything is excellent or praiseworthy—think about such things." Embracing self-belief involves cultivating thoughts and beliefs that are affirming, constructive, and aligned with God's truth, leading to increased joy and emotional resilience.

6. Influencing Interactions and Relationships: Self-belief also influences how individuals interact with others and form relationships. In Matthew 22:39 (NIV), Jesus teaches, "Love your neighbor as yourself." This instruction underscores the importance of self-love and self-respect as the foundation for healthy interactions. Embracing self-belief allows individuals to establish genuine connections, assert boundaries, and contribute positively to their communities.

In conclusion, embracing the power of self-belief is a transformative journey that aligns with biblical principles and empowers individuals to realize their full potential. By recognizing inner worth, overcoming limiting beliefs, fostering resilience, pursuing goals, cultivating a positive mindset, and enhancing relationships, self-belief becomes a driving force for personal growth, purposeful living, and a deep connection with God's plan. As individuals embrace their unique gifts and embrace self-belief, they embark on a journey of empowerment, resilience, and fulfillment.

Embracing the power of self-belief is a profound and transformative journey that aligns with both personal growth principles and the teachings of the Bible. It involves recognizing and harnessing the innate potential within oneself, cultivating a positive and empowering mindset, and embracing the truth of God's love and purpose for each individual.

1. Recognizing God's Creation: At the core of embracing the power of self-belief is the understanding that each person is fearfully and wonderfully made by God. Psalm 139:14 (NIV) declares, "I praise you because I am fearfully and wonderfully made; your works are wonderful, I know that full well." This verse emphasizes the divine craftsmanship that has gone into creating every individual. Embracing self-belief involves acknowledging this divine truth and understanding that God has endowed each person with unique talents, abilities, and potential.

2. Overcoming Doubt and Fear: Self-belief empowers individuals to overcome doubt and fear, recognizing that they are not alone in their journey. In Isaiah 41:10 (NIV), God reassures, "So do not fear, for I am with you; do not be dismayed, for I am your God. I will strengthen you and help you; I will uphold you with my righteous right hand." Embracing self-belief involves trusting in God's presence and strength, which enables individuals to face challenges with confidence and courage.

3. Aligning with God's Promises: Embracing self-belief involves aligning one's thoughts and beliefs with God's promises. In Jeremiah 29:11 (NIV), God declares, "'For I know the plans I have for you,' declares the Lord, 'plans to prosper you and not to harm you, plans to give you hope and a future.'" This promise reminds individuals that they are part of God's divine plan, instilling a sense of purpose and hope. By embracing self-belief, individuals trust that God's plan for them is full of blessings and opportunities.

4. Pursuing God-Given Dreams: Self-belief empowers individuals to pursue their God-given dreams and passions. In Philippians 4:13 (NIV), the apostle Paul proclaims, "I can do all this through him who gives me strength." This verse highlights the power of Christ's strength within believers. Embracing self-belief involves relying on God's strength to overcome obstacles and pursue dreams that align with His purpose.

5. Fostering a Positive Identity: Cultivating self-belief involves fostering a positive self-identity rooted in God's love. In 1 John 3:1 (NIV), it is written, "See what great love the Father has lavished on us, that we should be called children of God! And that is what we are!" This verse emphasizes the unconditional love and identity believers have as children of God. Embracing self-belief requires recognizing this identity and viewing oneself through the lens of God's love.

6. Embracing Resilience and Perseverance: Self-belief empowers individuals to embrace resilience and perseverance in the face of challenges. Romans 5:3-4 (NIV) explains, "Not only so, but we also glory in our sufferings, because we know that suffering produces perseverance; perseverance, character; and character, hope." This passage emphasizes the growth that arises from enduring challenges. Embracing self-belief involves seeing difficulties as opportunities for personal and spiritual development.

In conclusion, embracing the power of self-belief is a transformative journey that aligns with biblical truths and empowers individuals to reach their full potential. By recognizing God's creation, overcoming doubt, aligning with His promises, pursuing dreams, fostering a positive identity, and embracing resilience, individuals can develop a deep sense of self-worth and purpose. Through self-belief rooted in God's love and truth, individuals can navigate life's challenges with confidence, courage, and a steadfast faith in His plan.

2.3 Letting go of perfectionism

Letting Go of Perfectionism: Embracing Imperfection for Growth and Fulfillment

Perfectionism, a relentless pursuit of flawlessness, can be both a driving force and a hindrance in one's life. While striving for excellence and setting high standards can yield positive results, the unattainable quest for perfection often leads to stress, anxiety, and an inability to appreciate one's achievements. Letting go of perfectionism is a transformative journey that involves embracing imperfection, cultivating self-compassion, and redefining success to find genuine fulfillment and personal growth.

Understanding Perfectionism: The Illusion of Control

Perfectionism often stems from a desire for control and a fear of failure. In a world where the pressure to succeed is palpable, individuals may believe that attaining perfection will shield them from criticism and disappointment. However, this pursuit becomes a double-edged sword. While it may seem like a means of achieving success, it can also result in procrastination, self-doubt, and a constant feeling of inadequacy.

Perfectionism can manifest in various aspects of life, from academic and professional pursuits to personal relationships and self-image. The need to appear flawless and faultless becomes a heavy burden, hindering authentic self-expression and preventing individuals from taking risks that could lead to personal growth.

Embracing Imperfection: A Path to Authenticity

Letting go of perfectionism begins with embracing imperfection as a natural and human quality. Just as nature's beauty lies in its diversity and uniqueness, human beings are beautifully imperfect. Recognizing that no one is without flaws or mistakes frees individuals from the suffocating grip of perfectionism.

In 2 Corinthians 12:9-10 (NIV), the apostle Paul acknowledges the acceptance of imperfection: "But he said to me, 'My grace is sufficient for you, for my power is made perfect in weakness.' Therefore, I will boast all the more gladly about my weaknesses, so that Christ's power may rest on me. That is why, for Christ's sake, I delight in weaknesses, in insults, in hardships, in persecutions, in difficulties. For when I am weak, then I am strong." Paul's words highlight the paradox of strength emerging from vulnerability and imperfection, reinforcing the idea that embracing weaknesses can lead to profound growth.

Cultivating Self-Compassion: Nurturing the Inner Self

One of the pillars of letting go of perfectionism is self-compassion—a practice rooted in treating oneself with the same kindness and understanding as one would offer a dear friend. Rather than harsh self-criticism, self-compassion involves acknowledging mistakes and setbacks with empathy and a willingness to learn.

In Matthew 22:39 (NIV), Jesus teaches, "Love your neighbor as yourself." This principle emphasizes the importance of self-love and compassion as a foundation for healthy relationships with others. Letting go of perfectionism involves extending this love and compassion inward, recognizing that self-worth is not contingent on flawless performance.

Redefining Success: Embracing Growth and Learning

Perfectionism often leads to a rigid definition of success—one that is centered on external validation and flawless achievement. However, true success is a dynamic and personal concept that encompasses growth, resilience, and the courage to step outside one's comfort zone.

In Philippians 3:12-14 (NIV), Paul speaks about the pursuit of growth and progress: "Not that I have already obtained all this, or have already arrived at my goal, but I press on to take hold of that for which Christ Jesus took hold of me. Brothers and sisters, I do not consider myself yet to have taken hold of it. But one thing I do: Forgetting what is behind and straining toward what is ahead, I press on toward the goal to win the prize for which God has called me heavenward in Christ Jesus." Paul's words underscore the importance of continuous growth and the pursuit of purpose, even in the face of imperfection.

Embracing Vulnerability: A Source of Connection

Letting go of perfectionism involves embracing vulnerability—the willingness to show one's true self, including strengths and weaknesses. Vulnerability fosters authentic connections with others, as it allows for genuine interactions free from the constraints of maintaining a flawless facade.

In Galatians 6:2 (NIV), the Bible teaches about sharing burdens: "Carry each other's burdens, and in this way, you will fulfill the law of Christ." This principle highlights the importance of mutual support and understanding. Letting go of perfectionism enables individuals to reach out for help and connect on a deeper level, fostering a sense of belonging and shared humanity.

Finding Joy in Progress: A Lifelong Journey

Letting go of perfectionism is not a one-time achievement but a continuous journey. It involves celebrating progress, no matter how small, and reframing setbacks as opportunities for learning and growth. By embracing imperfection, practicing self-compassion, redefining success, embracing vulnerability, and finding joy in the journey, individuals can break free from the chains of perfectionism and embark on a path of authentic self-discovery and genuine fulfillment.

In conclusion, letting go of perfectionism is a liberating and transformative endeavor that aligns with the teachings of the Bible. By embracing imperfection, cultivating self-compassion, redefining success, embracing vulnerability, and finding joy in progress, individuals can experience a profound shift in their mindset and well-being. This journey allows for greater authenticity, connection, and personal growth, ultimately leading to a more fulfilled and purposeful life.

Letting Go of Perfectionism: A Biblical Perspective on Embracing Imperfection for Wholeness and Growth

Perfectionism, often driven by societal pressures and personal expectations, can become a formidable obstacle on the journey of self-discovery, personal growth, and spiritual fulfillment. While striving for excellence is commendable, the unrelenting pursuit of flawlessness can lead to stress, anxiety, and a distorted self-image. Letting go of perfectionism is a transformative process that aligns with biblical principles and involves embracing imperfection, cultivating grace, and recognizing the importance of genuine connection.

1. Recognizing Human Imperfection

At the heart of letting go of perfectionism is the recognition of human imperfection. The Bible acknowledges the fallibility of humanity and the need for God's grace. Romans 3:23 (NIV) reminds us, "For all have sinned and fall short of the glory of God." This verse underscores the universal truth that no one is without flaws. Embracing imperfection is not a sign of weakness, but an acknowledgment of our shared humanity and dependence on God's mercy.

2. God's Strength in Weakness

Letting go of perfectionism requires a shift in focus from self-reliance to reliance on God's strength. In 2 Corinthians 12:9-10 (NIV), the apostle Paul shares his revelation from God: "But he said to me, 'My grace is sufficient for you, for my power is made perfect in weakness.' Therefore, I will boast all the more gladly about my weaknesses, so that Christ's power may rest on me. That is why, for Christ's sake, I delight in weaknesses, in insults, in hardships, in persecutions, in difficulties. For when I am weak, then I am strong." Paul's words highlight the transformative power of God's grace and strength working through human weaknesses.

3. Cultivating Humility

Perfectionism often stems from pride and a desire for self-glory. Proverbs 16:18 (NIV) warns, "Pride goes before destruction, a haughty spirit before a fall." Letting go of perfectionism involves cultivating humility—recognizing our limitations and placing our trust in God's wisdom and providence. Humility allows us to release the need to control every outcome and surrender to God's perfect plan.

4. Embracing Forgiveness and Redemption

Perfectionism can create an unending cycle of self-criticism and guilt. However, the Bible emphasizes God's forgiveness and redemption. Psalm 103:12 (NIV) assures us, "As far as the east is from the west, so far has he removed our transgressions from us." Embracing imperfection involves accepting God's forgiveness and extending it to ourselves. It is a reminder that our worth is not determined by our mistakes, but by God's unchanging love.

5. Prioritizing Authentic Relationships

Letting go of perfectionism enables us to build authentic and meaningful relationships. Romans 15:7 (NIV) encourages us to, "Accept one another, then, just as Christ accepted you, in order to bring praise to God." When we let go of the need to appear flawless, we create space for genuine connection. Vulnerability and authenticity foster deeper relationships based on mutual understanding and empathy.

6. Finding Contentment in God

Perfectionism often leads to a constant striving for more, never truly experiencing contentment. Philippians 4:11-12 (NIV) offers a different perspective: "I am not saying this because I am in need, for I have learned to be content whatever the circumstances. I know what it is to be in need, and I know what it is to have plenty. I have learned the secret of being content in any and every situation, whether well fed or hungry, whether living in plenty or in want." Letting go of perfectionism involves finding contentment in God's presence and recognizing that true fulfillment comes from a relationship with Him, not from external achievements.

Letting go of perfectionism is a transformative journey that aligns with biblical teachings. By embracing imperfection, relying on God's strength, cultivating humility, accepting forgiveness, prioritizing authentic relationships, and finding contentment in God, individuals can break free from the chains of perfectionism. This journey leads to a deeper understanding of God's grace, a more genuine connection with others, and a greater sense of wholeness and spiritual fulfillment. Ultimately, letting go of perfectionism allows us to fully embrace our identity as beloved children of God, uniquely imperfect yet perfectly loved.

2.4 The role of self-compassion in overcoming fear

The Role of Self-Compassion in Overcoming Fear: Nurturing Inner Resilience and Empowerment

Fear is a powerful and primal emotion that can grip our hearts and minds, often hindering personal growth, decision-making, and well-being. Whether it's fear of failure, rejection, or the unknown, these anxieties can become formidable barriers to leading a fulfilling life. Self-compassion, a practice rooted in treating oneself with kindness and understanding, plays a crucial role in overcoming fear by nurturing inner resilience, fostering emotional well-being, and empowering individuals to face their fears with courage.

1. Embracing Imperfection and Humanity

At the core of self-compassion is the acknowledgment of our shared humanity and inherent imperfection. Fear often arises from a belief in our inadequacies or the potential for failure. However, self-compassion invites us to approach ourselves with the same gentleness and understanding that we would offer to a friend facing similar challenges. This perspective shift allows us to recognize that experiencing fear is a natural part of being human, rather than a sign of weakness.

2. Alleviating Self-Criticism and Judgment

Fear can be exacerbated by harsh self-criticism and negative self-talk. Self-compassion counteracts this pattern by replacing self-judgment with self-kindness. Instead of berating ourselves for feeling afraid, we treat ourselves with warmth and understanding. As Galatians 5:22-23 (NIV) reminds us, "But the fruit of the Spirit is love, joy, peace, forbearance, kindness, goodness, faithfulness, gentleness and self-control." Self-compassion aligns with the values of kindness and gentleness, fostering a nurturing inner environment that soothes fear and anxiety.

3. Cultivating Resilience

Self-compassion contributes to the development of emotional resilience—a key quality in overcoming fear. Romans 8:37 (NIV) declares, "No, in all these things we are more than conquerors through him who loved us." This verse emphasizes our capacity to overcome challenges through Christ's love. Similarly, self-compassion enables us to confront fear with a mindset of resilience and courage. By acknowledging our struggles without self-criticism, we become better equipped to navigate difficulties and emerge stronger on the other side.

4. Reducing Avoidance Behaviors

Fear often triggers avoidance behaviors, where we steer clear of situations or experiences that trigger discomfort. Self-compassion empowers us to face our fears head-on, knowing that we can offer ourselves kindness and support regardless of the outcome. This aligns with Psalm 23:4 (NIV): "Even though I walk through the darkest valley, I will fear no evil, for you are with me; your rod and your staff, they comfort me." With self-compassion as our ally, we can walk through the valleys of fear with a sense of comfort and inner strength.

5. Enhancing Self-Efficacy

Self-compassion bolsters self-efficacy—the belief in one's ability to navigate challenges successfully. 2 Timothy 1:7 (NIV) states, "For the Spirit God gave us does not make us timid, but gives us power, love and self-discipline." Self-compassion empowers us with love and self-discipline, counteracting the timidity that fear can instill. By acknowledging our fears without judgment and extending compassion to ourselves, we cultivate a sense of empowerment that fuels our confidence in facing and overcoming challenges.

6. Nurturing Inner Courage

Courage is not the absence of fear but the ability to act despite it. Self-compassion nurtures the inner courage needed to confront fear and take meaningful action. In Joshua 1:9 (NIV), God reassures, "Have I not commanded you? Be strong and courageous. Do not be afraid; do not be discouraged, for the Lord your God will be with you wherever you go." Self-compassion echoes this sentiment by reminding us that we are not alone in our fears. With self-compassion, we tap into a wellspring of inner strength that empowers us to face fear with courage and determination.

Self-compassion is a powerful antidote to fear, offering a path to inner resilience, emotional well-being, and empowerment. By embracing imperfection, alleviating self-criticism, cultivating resilience, reducing avoidance behaviors, enhancing self-efficacy, and nurturing inner courage, self-compassion equips individuals to confront their fears with grace and strength. Just as God's love and presence provide comfort and assurance, self-compassion becomes a steadfast companion in the journey to overcome fear and embrace life's challenges with a heart full of courage.

The Role of Self-Compassion in Overcoming Fear: Biblical Insights and Empowerment

Fear is a universal emotion that can hinder personal growth, decision-making, and well-being. It often stems from a sense of inadequacy or uncertainty, leading to avoidance and paralysis. Self-compassion, rooted in treating oneself with kindness and understanding, plays a vital role in overcoming fear by nurturing inner resilience, fostering emotional well-being, and empowering individuals to face their fears with courage, drawing insights from biblical teachings.

1. Embracing God's Love and Compassion

Self-compassion aligns with the biblical principle of God's boundless love and compassion for His children. Psalm 103:13-14 (NIV) says, "As a father has compassion on his children, so the Lord has compassion on those who fear him; for he knows how we are formed, he remembers that we are dust." Embracing self-compassion involves recognizing that, just as God is compassionate toward us, we too can show ourselves kindness and understanding, especially in times of fear and vulnerability.

2. Casting Anxiety on God

Fear often leads to anxiety, which can be alleviated through self-compassion and trust in God's care. 1 Peter 5:7 (NIV) advises, "Cast all your anxiety on him because he cares for you." Practicing self-compassion allows us to cast our fears and anxieties on God while treating ourselves with the same care and concern. This alignment with God's care empowers us to navigate fear with a sense of inner peace.

3. Resting in God's Strength

Self-compassion involves acknowledging our limitations and finding strength in God's power. Isaiah 41:10 (NIV) reassures, "So do not fear, for I am with you; do not be dismayed, for I am your God. I will strengthen you and help you; I will uphold you with my righteous right hand." Letting go of perfectionism and embracing self-compassion enables us to rest in God's strength, knowing that He supports us even in our moments of fear.

4. Overcoming Inadequacy through Grace

Feelings of inadequacy often fuel fear, but self-compassion can counteract this by embracing God's grace. Ephesians 2:8-9 (NIV) declares, "For it is by grace you have been saved, through faith—and this is not from yourselves, it is the gift of God—not by works, so that no one can boast." Similarly, self-compassion teaches us that our worth is not based on achieving perfection but on the grace of God. By extending grace to ourselves, we can overcome the paralyzing grip of inadequacy and fear.

5. Cultivating Confidence through God's Promises

Self-compassion empowers individuals to face fear with confidence, grounded in the promises of God. Joshua 1:9 (NIV) encourages, "Have I not commanded you? Be strong and courageous. Do not be afraid; do not be discouraged, for the Lord your God will be with you wherever you go." Self-compassion reinforces the belief that God's presence is a source of strength and courage, enabling us to confront fear with faith and determination.

6. Practicing Wisdom and Sound Mind

Fear often distorts our thinking, but self-compassion aligns with the biblical call to sound judgment and wisdom. 2 Timothy 1:7 (NIV) states, "For the Spirit God gave us does not make us timid, but gives us power, love and self-discipline." Self-compassion fosters self-discipline by promoting healthy self-care and self-talk, leading to a clearer and calmer mind in the face of fear.

Conclusion

Self-compassion, deeply rooted in God's love and biblical teachings, is a transformative tool for overcoming fear. Through embracing God's compassion, casting anxieties on Him, resting in His strength, embracing grace, cultivating confidence in His promises, and practicing sound judgment, self-compassion empowers individuals to navigate fear with resilience and courage. Just as God's love and wisdom guide us through challenges, self-compassion becomes a tangible expression of His grace in our journey to overcome fear and embrace life's uncertainties with unwavering faith.

CHAPTER THREE
SETTING REALISTIC GOALS

Setting Realistic Goals:

Setting realistic goals is a fundamental practice that plays a crucial role in achieving personal growth, success, and fulfillment. It involves identifying achievable objectives that align with one's capabilities, resources, and circumstances. By setting realistic goals, individuals can harness motivation, maintain focus, and experience a sense of accomplishment while avoiding the pitfalls of overambition and disappointment.

1. Assessing Personal Capabilities: Setting realistic goals begins with a thorough assessment of one's strengths, skills, and limitations. It involves recognizing one's current level of expertise and understanding what is feasible given existing knowledge and abilities. This self-awareness enables individuals to set goals that challenge them without setting unrealistic expectations.

2. Considering Resources and Constraints: Realistic goal-setting takes into account available resources, including time, energy, finances, and support. It acknowledges potential constraints and ensures that goals can be pursued within the parameters of one's daily life and commitments. By considering these factors, individuals can avoid setting goals that may be impractical or unsustainable.

3. Defining Clear and Measurable Objectives: Realistic goals are specific, measurable, achievable, relevant, and time-bound (SMART). Clarity in goal definition provides a roadmap for action, making it easier to track progress and measure success. For example, a goal to "exercise for 30 minutes three times a week" is more concrete and attainable than a vague goal like "get fit."

4. Balancing Aspirations and Reality: Setting realistic goals involves finding a balance between aspirations and the current reality. While it's important to dream big and aim high, it's equally crucial to ground those aspirations in practical steps. This approach prevents individuals from becoming discouraged by overly ambitious goals that seem out of reach.

5. Maintaining Motivation and Focus: Realistic goals are more likely to inspire and maintain motivation. Achieving incremental successes reinforces a sense of accomplishment and provides the drive to continue pursuing larger objectives. This aligns with Proverbs 13:4 (NIV), which states, "A sluggard's appetite is never filled, but the desires of the diligent are fully satisfied." Diligence in pursuing achievable goals leads to a sense of satisfaction and fulfillment.

6. Cultivating Self-Discipline: Setting realistic goals fosters self-discipline and consistency. When goals are manageable and attainable, individuals are more likely to commit to the necessary actions and routines. This resonates with 1 Corinthians 9:24 (NIV): "Do you not know that in a race all the runners run, but only one gets the prize? Run in such a way as to get the prize." Setting achievable goals enables individuals to "run" with purpose and determination.

7. Minimizing Stress and Overwhelm: Unrealistic goals can lead to stress, burnout, and a sense of overwhelm. Setting achievable goals reduces these negative effects by breaking down larger objectives into manageable steps. By following a gradual progression, individuals can avoid becoming overwhelmed and maintain a healthy work-life balance.

8. Celebrating Achievements: Realistic goals provide opportunities for regular celebration of achievements. Each milestone reached serves as a testament to dedication and effort. This aligns with

Philippians 4:13 (NIV): "I can do all this through him who gives me strength." Celebrating successes acknowledges the role of God's strength in enabling us to achieve our goals.

Accordingly, setting realistic goals is a practical and effective approach to personal growth and achievement. By assessing personal capabilities, considering resources, defining clear objectives, balancing aspirations with reality, maintaining motivation, cultivating self-discipline, minimizing stress, and celebrating achievements, individuals can navigate their journey with purpose and intention. Just as the Bible encourages stewardship of talents and diligence in pursuing goals, setting realistic goals empowers individuals to embark on a path of continuous improvement and success while embracing their unique journey of growth.

Biblical Lense:

Setting realistic goals is a strategic and spiritually grounded practice that involves identifying achievable objectives in alignment with one's abilities, resources, and divine purpose. This intentional approach not only fosters personal growth and success but also reflects biblical principles of stewardship, perseverance, and trust in God's guidance.

1. Stewardship of Talents: Setting realistic goals is an act of stewardship, acknowledging the unique talents and gifts that God has bestowed upon each individual. Matthew 25:14-15 (NIV) illustrates the concept of stewardship: "Again, it will be like a man going on a journey, who called his servants and entrusted his wealth to them. To one he gave five bags of gold, to another two bags, and to another one bag, each according to his ability." Just as the servants were entrusted with different amounts of wealth, individuals are entrusted with varying talents. Setting achievable goals allows for the responsible and purposeful use of these gifts.

2. Trusting in God's Plan: Proverbs 16:9 (NIV) reminds us, "In their hearts humans plan their course, but the Lord establishes their steps." While setting goals involves planning, it is essential to recognize God's role in guiding our paths. Setting realistic goals involves aligning our aspirations with God's will, acknowledging that His divine plan may differ from our initial expectations. Trusting in His guidance ensures that our goals are harmonious with His purpose for our lives.

3. Diligence and Perseverance: Setting realistic goals encourages diligent effort and perseverance, reflecting biblical values. Hebrews 12:1 (NIV) compares life to a race: "Therefore, since we are surrounded by

such a great cloud of witnesses, let us throw off everything that hinders and the sin that so easily entangles. And let us run with perseverance the race marked out for us." Just as athletes train and persevere to reach the finish line, setting achievable goals requires consistent effort and determination.

4. Recognizing Limitations: Ecclesiastes 3:1 (NIV) states, "There is a time for everything, and a season for every activity under the heavens." Setting realistic goals involves recognizing the seasons of life and acknowledging personal limitations. While God's grace empowers us, embracing our human limitations is an act of humility. By setting goals that consider these limitations, we honor the balance between ambition and practicality.

5. Contentment and Gratitude: Philippians 4:11-12 (NIV) emphasizes contentment: "I am not saying this because I am in need, for I have learned to be content whatever the circumstances. I know what it is to be in need, and I know what it is to have plenty." Setting realistic goals promotes contentment by focusing on attainable objectives rather than constantly striving for more. This aligns with the practice of gratitude for the blessings we have.

6. Wise Planning and Foresight: Proverbs 21:5 (NIV) states, "The plans of the diligent lead to profit as surely as haste leads to poverty." Setting realistic goals involves diligent planning and wise decision-making. It encourages individuals to consider the potential outcomes of their actions and make informed choices that contribute to their overall well-being.

7. Rejoicing in Progress: Celebrating progress is an integral part of setting realistic goals. Proverbs 15:23 (NIV) highlights the joy in achieving milestones: "A person finds joy in giving an apt reply—and how good is a timely word!" Each step toward an achievable goal can be viewed as a timely word of progress, inviting us to rejoice and give thanks for the journey.

Conclusion: Setting realistic goals is a purposeful and faith-filled endeavor that aligns with biblical principles. By practicing stewardship of talents, trusting in God's plan, demonstrating diligence and perseverance, recognizing limitations, fostering contentment, engaging in wise planning, and rejoicing in progress, individuals embark on a journey of growth that honors both their unique gifts and God's divine guidance. Through this balanced approach, individuals can cultivate a life of purpose, success, and spiritual fulfillment.

3.1 The importance of clarity and purpose

The Importance of Clarity and Purpose: Navigating Life with Intention and Fulfillment

Clarity and purpose are two fundamental pillars that provide direction, meaning, and fulfillment to our lives. These elements serve as guiding beacons, helping us navigate the complexities of our journey, make informed decisions, and achieve a sense of accomplishment. By fostering clarity in our goals and aligning them with a meaningful purpose, we unlock the potential for growth, resilience, and a profound sense of well-being.

1. Clarity: Illuminating the Path

Clarity refers to the clear understanding of our goals, aspirations, and the steps needed to reach them. When we possess clarity, we are equipped with a vivid mental image of our desired outcomes. This mental clarity acts as a compass, guiding our actions and choices toward the realization of our goals. Just as Proverbs 4:25 (NIV) advises, "Let your eyes look straight ahead; fix your gaze directly before you." Clarity enables us to keep our focus fixed on the path ahead, avoiding distractions and detours.

2. Setting Goals and Objectives

Clarity is essential in setting well-defined goals and objectives. It enables us to articulate what we want to achieve, breaking down broad visions into actionable steps. Goals become more attainable when we can clearly see the milestones we need to reach along the way. This approach resonates with Philippians 3:13-14 (NIV): "Forgetting what is behind and straining toward what is ahead, I press on toward the goal to win the prize for which God has called me heavenward in Christ Jesus." Clarity empowers us to press forward with purpose and determination.

3. Informed Decision-Making

Clarity facilitates informed decision-making by providing a framework to evaluate choices against our desired outcomes. When we possess a clear sense of purpose, we can assess whether a decision aligns with our goals and values. This discernment process is reminiscent of James 1:5 (NIV): "If any of you lacks wisdom, you should ask God, who gives generously to all without finding fault, and it will be given to you." Clarity enables us to seek and receive wisdom to make choices that propel us closer to our purpose.

4. Focus and Productivity

Clarity enhances focus and productivity. With a clear vision of our goals, we can allocate our time, energy, and resources efficiently.

We avoid spreading ourselves too thin and ensure that our efforts are directed toward tasks that contribute to our overarching purpose. Colossians 3:23-24 (NIV) reminds us, "Whatever you do, work at it with all your heart, as working for the Lord, not for human masters, since you know that you will receive an inheritance from the Lord as a reward." Clarity enables us to work with dedication and purpose, maximizing our impact.

5. Meaning and Fulfillment

A life marked by clarity and purpose is inherently meaningful and fulfilling. When we understand our goals and the reasons behind our actions, we experience a sense of alignment between our intentions and our achievements. This congruence resonates with Psalms 90:17 (NIV): "May the favor of the Lord our God rest on us; establish the work of our hands for us—yes, establish the work of our hands." Clarity and purpose bestow divine favor upon our endeavors, infusing our actions with a sense of significance.

6. Resilience and Adaptability

Clarity and purpose provide a foundation of resilience and adaptability. When challenges arise, individuals with a clear sense of purpose are more likely to persevere and navigate obstacles. Romans 8:28 (NIV) offers solace in this regard: "And we know that in all things God works for the good of those who love him, who have been called according to his purpose." Clarity empowers us to trust that even in adversity, our efforts are part of a greater purpose that transcends difficulties.

Conclusion

Clarity and purpose are twin forces that guide us toward a life of intention, meaning, and fulfillment. Through clarity, we gain a focused vision of our goals and the steps needed to achieve them. This clarity empowers us to make informed decisions, stay focused, and experience a sense of accomplishment. When aligned with purpose, our actions become imbued with deeper meaning and divine favor. This combination of clarity and purpose not only propels us forward but also equips us with the resilience needed to overcome challenges. Ultimately, a life driven by clarity and purpose is a journey marked by intentionality, growth, and a profound sense of well-being.

The Importance of Clarity and Purpose: Guiding Life's Journey with Biblical Wisdom

Clarity and purpose serve as guiding lights on the intricate path of life, illuminating the way forward and infusing each step with meaning. These foundational principles, deeply rooted in biblical teachings, empower individuals to navigate challenges, make wise decisions, and experience a profound sense of fulfillment as they align their aspirations with divine guidance.

1. Clarity: A Vision Unveiled

Clarity, often referred to as a "clear vision," involves the ability to see one's goals and aspirations with precision. Proverbs 29:18 (NIV) underscores the significance of clarity: "Where there is no revelation, people cast off restraint; but blessed is the one who heeds wisdom's instruction." When we possess clarity, we heed wisdom's instruction, enabling us to set focused and purposeful goals that align with God's plan for our lives.

2. Purpose: Anchoring the Heart

Purpose is the anchoring force that gives meaning to our pursuits and decisions. Romans 8:28 (NIV) assures us, "And we know that in all things God works for the good of those who love him, who have been called according to his purpose." This verse highlights how our endeavors, when driven by God's purpose, are woven into a tapestry of divine providence. A life rooted in purpose is a life that harmonizes with God's intentions for us.

3. Alignment with God's Will

Clarity and purpose are intertwined with the concept of seeking God's will. Proverbs 3:5-6 (NIV) implores us, "Trust in the Lord with all your heart and lean not on your own understanding; in all your ways submit to him, and he will make your paths straight." This submission to God's guidance brings clarity to our decisions, ensuring that our steps are aligned with His purpose for our lives.

4. Navigating Decisions

Clarity and purpose provide a compass for decision-making. James 1:5 (NIV) emphasizes seeking wisdom: "If any of you lacks wisdom, you should ask God, who gives generously to all without finding fault, and it will be given to you." This divine wisdom clarifies our choices and leads us to decisions that honor our purpose and contribute to our growth.

5. Resilience in Challenges

A life rooted in clarity and purpose offers resilience in the face of trials. James 1:2-4 (NIV) states, "Consider it pure joy, my brothers and sisters, whenever you face trials of many kinds, because you know that the testing of your faith produces perseverance. Let perseverance finish its work so that you may be mature and complete, not lacking anything." Clarity about our purpose bolsters our perseverance, transforming challenges into opportunities for growth.

6. Cultivating Gratitude

Clarity and purpose foster gratitude for the journey. Psalm 90:12 (NIV) implores, "Teach us to number our days, that we may gain a heart of wisdom." When we embrace clarity and purpose, we become attuned to the preciousness of each moment. This awareness cultivates gratitude for the steps we take, regardless of their size, knowing that they contribute to the greater purpose set before us.

7. Impact and Legacy

Living with clarity and purpose allows us to leave a lasting impact. Ephesians 2:10 (NIV) affirms, "For we are God's handiwork, created in Christ Jesus to do good works, which God prepared in advance for us to do." By embracing our purpose and aligning it with God's plan, we become instruments of His work, leaving a legacy that extends beyond our individual lives.

Conclusion

Clarity and purpose are not mere concepts but essential pillars that underpin a life of intention, fulfillment, and divine alignment. Grounded in biblical wisdom, they guide us in setting meaningful goals, making wise decisions, weathering challenges, and leaving a lasting impact. As we embrace clarity of vision and align our purpose with God's plan, we embark on a transformative journey that leads to a life of significance, joy, and spiritual abundance.

3.2 Breaking down big goals into manageable steps

Breaking Down Big Goals into Manageable Steps: The Art of Progress and Achievement

Big goals, while inspiring and ambitious, can often feel overwhelming and unattainable when viewed as a whole. Breaking them down into manageable steps is a strategic approach that not only facilitates progress but also enhances motivation, minimizes stress, and increases the likelihood of success. This practice involves dissecting complex objectives into smaller, actionable tasks, aligning with the principles of planning, perseverance, and stewardship.

1. Clarity and Focus

Breaking down big goals provides clarity and focus. Just as Proverbs 4:25 (NIV) advises, "Let your eyes look straight ahead; fix your gaze directly before you," this approach helps individuals direct their attention toward specific, achievable tasks. Smaller steps create a clear path to follow, reducing the sense of overwhelm and allowing for concentrated effort.

2. Overcoming Overwhelm

Large goals can evoke feelings of overwhelm and anxiety, hindering progress. Breaking them into manageable steps transforms a daunting endeavor into a series of achievable milestones. This aligns with Philippians 4:6-7 (NIV): "Do not be anxious about anything, but in every situation, by prayer and petition, with thanksgiving, present your requests to God. And the peace of God, which transcends all understanding, will guard your hearts and your minds in Christ Jesus." By taking one step at a time, individuals experience a sense of peace and focused purpose.

3. Building Momentum

Breaking down big goals into smaller steps creates a sense of momentum. Each completed task becomes a building block, propelling individuals forward. This sense of progress fosters motivation and aligns with Proverbs 13:4 (NIV): "A sluggard's appetite is never filled, but the desires of the diligent are fully satisfied." Diligent effort in achieving smaller tasks satisfies the appetite for progress, encouraging consistent action.

4. Celebrating Achievements

Reaching smaller milestones provides opportunities for celebration. Proverbs 15:23 (NIV) affirms, "A person finds joy in giving an apt reply—and how good is a timely word!" In the context of goal achievement, each completed step becomes a timely word of success. Celebrating these moments not only boosts morale but also fuels the desire to continue moving forward.

5. Enhanced Problem-Solving

Breaking down goals promotes problem-solving and adaptability. As challenges arise during the pursuit of smaller tasks, individuals develop creative solutions and learn valuable lessons. James 1:2-3 (NIV) encourages resilience: "Consider it pure joy, my brothers and sisters, whenever you face trials of many kinds, because you know that the testing of your faith produces perseverance." Overcoming challenges within manageable steps fosters perseverance and character growth.

6. Utilizing Time and Resources Efficiently

Breaking down goals allows for efficient allocation of time and resources. Instead of dedicating all efforts to a single massive objective, individuals can distribute their energy across smaller tasks. This aligns with Ecclesiastes 3:1 (NIV): "There is a time for everything, and a season for every activity under the heavens." Properly timing and organizing tasks optimize productivity.

7. Empowering Stewardship

Breaking down goals embodies the principle of stewardship. Just as in the parable of the talents (Matthew 25:14-30, NIV), effective stewardship involves wisely investing resources for growth. By breaking down goals, individuals invest their time and effort into manageable actions, maximizing their potential and growth.

Conclusion

Breaking down big goals into manageable steps is a strategic approach that aligns with biblical principles of planning, perseverance, and stewardship. This practice empowers individuals to navigate complexity, overcome overwhelm, build momentum, celebrate achievements, enhance problem-solving skills, utilize resources efficiently, and embrace effective stewardship. By taking incremental, purposeful steps, individuals embark on a journey of progress, achievement, and transformative growth, ultimately realizing the vision of their larger aspirations.

Breaking Down Big Goals into Manageable Steps: A Biblical Approach to Achievement and Progress

The process of breaking down big goals into manageable steps is a strategic and spiritually grounded approach that aligns with biblical principles of planning, diligence, and stewardship. By dissecting daunting objectives into smaller, actionable tasks, individuals can experience steady progress, overcome challenges, and fulfill their God-given potential.

1. Biblical Wisdom in Planning

Proverbs 21:5 (NIV) states, "The plans of the diligent lead to profit as surely as haste leads to poverty." Breaking down big goals reflects the wisdom of planning and diligent preparation. Just as a farmer cultivates the land step by step to yield a bountiful harvest, individuals break down their goals into smaller tasks to ensure steady growth and success.

2. Diligence and Perseverance

Proverbs 13:4 (NIV) highlights the importance of diligence: "A sluggard's appetite is never filled, but the desires of the diligent are fully satisfied." Breaking down goals encourages diligent effort, contributing to a sense of satisfaction and fulfillment as each smaller step is achieved. This practice cultivates perseverance and aligns with James 1:12 (NIV):

"Blessed is the one who perseveres under trial because, having stood the test, that person will receive the crown of life that the Lord has promised to those who love him."

3. Trusting God's Guidance

Proverbs 3:5-6 (NIV) emphasizes trust in God's guidance: "Trust in the Lord with all your heart and lean not on your own understanding; in all your ways submit to him, and he will make your paths straight." Breaking down goals involves submitting each step to God, acknowledging His sovereignty over our plans. By seeking His guidance, we align our efforts with His divine purpose.

4. Celebrating Milestones

In the parable of the talents (Matthew 25:14-30, NIV), the faithful stewards are commended for their faithful management of resources. Breaking down goals allows for the celebration of milestones along the way, resembling the master's words in Matthew 25:21 (NIV): "Well done, good and faithful servant! You have been faithful with a few things; I will put you in charge of many things. Come and share your master's happiness!" Each accomplished step becomes an opportunity to hear these words of affirmation.

5. Wisdom in Timing

Ecclesiastes 3:1 (NIV) acknowledges the importance of timing: "There is a time for everything, and a season for every activity under the heavens." Breaking down goals involves wisely allocating tasks to appropriate times, ensuring efficient use of resources. This aligns with the principle of stewardship, managing our time and efforts in a manner that honors God's design.

6. Overcoming Obstacles

In the face of challenges, breaking down goals provides a structured approach to problem-solving. James 1:2-4 (NIV) reminds us, "Consider it pure joy, my brothers and sisters, whenever you face trials of many kinds, because you know that the testing of your faith produces perseverance. Let perseverance finish its work so that you may be mature and complete, not lacking anything." By addressing challenges within smaller steps, individuals cultivate perseverance and spiritual maturity.

7. Fulfilling God's Purpose

Ephesians 2:10 (NIV) emphasizes the concept of purpose: "For we are God's handiwork, created in Christ Jesus to do good works, which God prepared in advance for us to do." Breaking down big goals into manageable steps aligns with this divine design, enabling us to fulfill the good works God has prepared for us. Each step contributes to the larger purpose that God has set before us.

Conclusion

Breaking down big goals into manageable steps is a holistic approach that combines practical wisdom with biblical principles. This strategy empowers individuals to plan diligently, persevere through challenges, celebrate milestones, trust in God's guidance, steward resources wisely, and fulfill their unique purpose. By aligning their efforts with God's design and seeking His guidance at each step, individuals embark on a journey of transformative growth, progress, and the realization of their God-given potential.

3.3 Embracing the process over the outcome

Embracing the Process Over the Outcome: A Journey of Growth and Spiritual Enrichment

In a world often fixated on results and achievements, the concept of embracing the process over the outcome offers a refreshing perspective that aligns with both personal growth and spiritual enrichment. This mindset encourages individuals to focus on the journey, the effort, and the lessons learned along the way, rather than being solely fixated on the end result. By prioritizing the process, individuals can experience deeper fulfillment, resilience, and a profound sense of purpose.

1. Learning and Growth

Embracing the process over the outcome fosters a mindset of continuous learning and growth. Just as 2 Peter 3:18 (NIV) encourages us to "grow in the grace and knowledge of our Lord and Savior Jesus Christ," the process-oriented approach invites us to appreciate each step of the journey as an opportunity for personal and spiritual development. It reminds us that challenges and setbacks are integral parts of growth, providing valuable lessons and insights.

2. Cultivating Resilience

The process-focused mindset cultivates resilience in the face of challenges and setbacks. James 1:2-4 (NIV) teaches, "Consider it pure joy, my brothers and sisters, whenever you face trials of many kinds, because you know that the testing of your faith produces perseverance. Let perseverance finish its work so that you may be mature and complete, not lacking anything." Embracing the process allows us to view trials as stepping stones to greater strength and maturity.

3. Presence and Mindfulness

Embracing the process encourages living in the present moment and practicing mindfulness. Philippians 4:6-7 (NIV) advises, "Do not be anxious about anything, but in every situation, by prayer and petition, with thanksgiving, present your requests to God. And the peace of God, which transcends all understanding, will guard your hearts and your minds in Christ Jesus." Focusing on the process enables us to fully engage with each moment, fostering a sense of peace and gratitude.

4. Celebrating Small Victories

The process-oriented approach allows for the celebration of small victories and milestones along the way. Proverbs 15:23 (NIV) states, "A person finds joy in giving an apt reply—and how good is a timely word!" Similarly, each step of progress becomes a "timely word" of achievement. Embracing these moments of growth and progress reinforces motivation and generates a sense of accomplishment.

5. Detachment from Perfectionism

Embracing the process over the outcome liberates individuals from the constraints of perfectionism. Ecclesiastes 7:20 (NIV) acknowledges human imperfection: "Indeed, there is no one on earth who is righteous, no one who does what is right and never sins." By accepting imperfection as a natural part of the process, individuals can pursue their goals with a healthier perspective and greater self-compassion.

6. Deepening Spiritual Connection

The process-focused mindset deepens one's spiritual connection by aligning with the concept of God's timing and divine plan. Isaiah 55:8-9 (NIV) affirms, "For my thoughts are not your thoughts, neither are your ways my ways, declares the Lord. As the heavens are higher than the earth, so are my ways higher than your ways and my thoughts than your thoughts." Embracing the process acknowledges that our understanding is limited, and God's plan unfolds gradually, often in ways that surpass our expectations.

7. Sustainable Joy and Fulfillment

In Matthew 6:34 (NIV), Jesus instructs, "Therefore do not worry about tomorrow, for tomorrow will worry about itself. Each day has enough trouble of its own." Embracing the process aligns with this teaching by inviting us to focus on the present moment and find joy in the journey. The satisfaction derived from engaging fully with the process leads to sustainable joy and lasting fulfillment.

Conclusion

Embracing the process over the outcome is a transformative approach that aligns with biblical principles of growth, resilience, mindfulness, and trust in God's plan. By valuing the journey, celebrating progress, and embracing imperfection, individuals can experience a deeper sense of purpose and fulfillment. This mindset encourages us to be present in each moment, learn from challenges, and recognize the divine wisdom that unfolds as we journey toward our goals. Ultimately, embracing the process empowers us to walk a path of personal and spiritual enrichment, drawing closer to our true potential and God's purpose for our lives.

Embracing the Process Over the Outcome: A Biblical Perspective on Growth and Contentment

In a world driven by instant gratification and a relentless pursuit of results, the concept of embracing the process over the outcome offers a profound shift in perspective that resonates with biblical teachings. This mindset encourages individuals to focus on the journey itself, valuing the lessons, character development, and spiritual enrichment that come from engaging wholeheartedly with the process. By prioritizing the process, we align with biblical principles of patience, trust, and contentment.

1. Patience and God's Timing

Embracing the process acknowledges the importance of God's timing. Ecclesiastes 3:1 (NIV) reminds us, "There is a time for everything, and a season for every activity under the heavens." This verse underscores that God orchestrates the various seasons of life, and our role is to embrace each moment as part of His divine plan. By focusing on the process, we cultivate patience and learn to trust in God's perfect timing.

2. Contentment in All Circumstances

Philippians 4:11-12 (NIV) emphasizes contentment: "I am not saying this because I am in need, for I have learned to be content whatever the circumstances. I know what it is to be in need, and I know what it is to have plenty." Embracing the process allows us to find contentment in the journey itself, regardless of the outcomes. It shifts our focus from external achievements to inner peace and satisfaction.

3. Lessons in Perseverance

The process-oriented mindset is closely tied to the concept of perseverance. James 1:12 (NIV) assures, "Blessed is the one who perseveres under trial because, having stood the test, that person will receive the crown of life that the Lord has promised to those who love him." Embracing the process means persevering through challenges, viewing them as opportunities for growth and character refinement.

4. Transformation and Renewal

Romans 12:2 (NIV) encourages transformation through the renewal of the mind: "Do not conform to the pattern of this world, but be transformed by the renewing of your mind. Then you will be able to test and approve what God's will is—his good, pleasing and perfect will." Embracing the process fosters this transformation as we allow our minds to be renewed by the experiences, insights, and growth that come from fully engaging with the journey.

5. Trusting God's Sovereignty

Proverbs 16:9 (NIV) affirms the importance of trusting in God's sovereignty: "In their hearts humans plan their course, but the Lord establishes their steps." When we embrace the process, we surrender our need for complete control and trust that God is guiding our steps. This aligns with Psalm 37:5 (NIV): "Commit your way to the Lord; trust in him and he will do this."

6. Present-Moment Awareness

Matthew 6:34 (NIV) teaches, "Therefore do not worry about tomorrow, for tomorrow will worry about itself. Each day has enough trouble of its own." Embracing the process invites us to focus on the present moment, fully immersing ourselves in the task at hand. This mindfulness aligns with the idea of seeking God's presence in each moment.

7. Fruitfulness through Abiding

In John 15:5 (NIV), Jesus uses the metaphor of a vine and branches to illustrate the importance of abiding in Him: "I am the vine; you are the branches. If you remain in me and I in you, you will bear much fruit; apart from me you can do nothing." Embracing the process involves abiding in Christ, recognizing that our growth and fruitfulness come from our connection with Him.

Conclusion

Embracing the process over the outcome is a transformative mindset that aligns with biblical principles of patience, trust, contentment, and growth. By valuing the journey, we learn to appreciate the lessons, character development, and spiritual enrichment that come from fully engaging with the process. This perspective empowers us to find joy and fulfillment in the present moment, trusting in God's timing and sovereignty, and cultivating a deeper connection with Him. As we embrace the process, we navigate life's challenges with resilience, celebrate the small victories, and ultimately discover a profound sense of purpose and spiritual abundance.

3.4 Celebrating small wins along the way

Celebrating Small Wins Along the Way: A Path to Motivation and Achievement

Celebrating small wins along the way is a powerful and transformative practice that harnesses the energy of progress, boosts motivation, and enhances the journey toward achieving larger goals. This approach involves acknowledging and appreciating even the smallest accomplishments, recognizing that each step forward contributes to the overall success. By infusing the process with positive reinforcement and gratitude, individuals can experience increased resilience, motivation, and a sense of fulfillment.

1. Recognizing Progress

Celebrating small wins allows individuals to recognize their progress, no matter how incremental it may seem. This acknowledgment aligns with Proverbs 24:16 (NIV): "for though the righteous fall seven times, they rise again, but the wicked stumble when calamity strikes." Each small victory is a testament to resilience and the ability to rise after setbacks, reinforcing a positive mindset.

2. Motivation and Momentum

Small wins generate a sense of motivation and momentum. Just as Proverbs 13:19 (NIV) describes the desire fulfilled as a tree of life, celebrating these moments creates a positive feedback loop. The motivation from a small victory propels individuals forward, building momentum and sustaining their drive to achieve more significant milestones.

3. Building Confidence

Celebrating small wins builds confidence and self-efficacy. 1 Corinthians 15:10 (NIV) reflects on God's grace empowering us: "But by the grace of God I am what I am, and his grace to me was not without effect. No, I worked harder than all of them—yet not I, but the grace of God that was with me." Each small win is a reminder of God's grace and our capacity for growth, bolstering our confidence in our abilities.

4. Fostering Perseverance

Small wins fuel perseverance in the face of challenges. Romans 5:3-4 (NIV) speaks of perseverance leading to character and hope: "Not only so, but we also glory in our sufferings, because we know that suffering produces perseverance; perseverance, character; and character, hope." By celebrating small victories, individuals develop the resilience needed to persevere through difficulties.

5. Cultivating Gratitude

The practice of celebrating small wins cultivates gratitude. 1 Thessalonians 5:18 (NIV) advises, "give thanks in all circumstances; for this is God's will for you in Christ Jesus." Gratitude amplifies the joy of achievements, fostering a positive mindset and nurturing a deeper connection with God.

6. Overcoming Overwhelm

Large goals can sometimes be overwhelming, but celebrating small wins breaks them into manageable pieces. Zechariah 4:10 (NIV) encourages, "Do not despise these small beginnings, for the Lord rejoices to see the work begin." Embracing small wins acknowledges the significance of each step and prevents the feeling of being overwhelmed by the entire journey.

7. Cultivating a Positive Mindset

Celebrating small wins contributes to a positive mindset. Philippians 4:8 (NIV) emphasizes the importance of focusing on positive and praiseworthy thoughts: "Finally, brothers and sisters, whatever is true, whatever is noble, whatever is right, whatever is pure, whatever is lovely, whatever is admirable—if anything is excellent or praiseworthy—think about such things." By celebrating achievements, individuals actively engage in cultivating a positive thought pattern.

Conclusion

Celebrating small wins along the way is a practice that aligns with biblical principles of gratitude, perseverance, motivation, and growth. By acknowledging and appreciating even the smallest achievements, individuals create a supportive environment for progress, motivation, and the development of a positive mindset. Each small victory is a testament to the journey's resilience, God's grace, and the capacity for growth. This practice empowers individuals to navigate challenges with confidence, sustain their motivation, and experience a profound sense of fulfillment as they journey toward their larger goals.

Celebrating Small Wins Along the Way: A Biblical Perspective on Gratitude and Progress

Celebrating small wins along the way is a transformative practice deeply rooted in biblical principles of gratitude, perseverance, and recognizing God's faithfulness in our journey. By embracing the habit of acknowledging and rejoicing in even the smallest accomplishments, individuals can experience increased motivation, a positive mindset, and a deeper connection with God's providence.

1. Gratitude for God's Blessings

Psalm 118:24 (NIV) encourages us with the words, "This is the day the Lord has made; let us rejoice and be glad in it." Celebrating small wins aligns with this sentiment, emphasizing gratitude for each day's blessings, progress, and achievements. By acknowledging even, the modest steps forward, we cultivate a heart of thankfulness that honors God's constant presence in our lives.

2. Perseverance and Faithfulness

James 1:12 (NIV) speaks of the reward for persevering under trial: "Blessed is the one who perseveres under trial because, having stood the test, that person will receive the crown of life that the Lord has promised to those who love him." Celebrating small wins reflects this perseverance, highlighting the faithfulness of God in guiding us through challenges and helping us overcome obstacles.

3. Joy in the Journey

Proverbs 15:23 (NIV) reminds us, "A person finds joy in giving an apt reply—and how good is a timely word!" Celebrating small wins brings timely words of joy into our journey. It enables us to find joy in the process itself, appreciating the incremental progress and milestones along the way.

4. Acknowledging Growth

Philippians 1:6 (NIV) assures us of God's ongoing work in our lives: "Being confident of this, that he who began a good work in you will carry it on to completion until the day of Christ Jesus." Celebrating small wins acknowledges the growth and transformation God is nurturing within us, affirming that each step forward is evidence of His work in our journey.

5. Overcoming Discouragement

Celebrating small wins serves as a shield against discouragement. Galatians 6:9 (NIV) encourages, "Let us not become weary in doing good, for at the proper time we will reap a harvest if we do not give up." When we celebrate small victories, we reinforce our resolve to persevere, guarding against the weariness that can hinder progress.

6. Renewed Focus on God

Colossians 3:17 (NIV) teaches, "And whatever you do, whether in word or deed, do it all in the name of the Lord Jesus, giving thanks to God the Father through him." By celebrating small wins, we redirect our focus toward God, recognizing His role in our achievements and offerings of gratitude.

7. Cultivating a Grateful Heart

1 Thessalonians 5:18 (NIV) instructs us, "give thanks in all circumstances; for this is God's will for you in Christ Jesus." Embracing the practice of celebrating small wins nurtures a grateful heart, in alignment with God's desire for us to recognize His blessings, both big and small.

Conclusion

Celebrating small wins along the way is a practice that intertwines biblical wisdom with the pursuit of personal growth. By embracing gratitude, perseverance, and joy in the journey, individuals can navigate challenges with renewed vigor and a positive mindset. Each small victory becomes a testament to God's faithfulness, our perseverance, and the transformative power of recognizing and rejoicing in even the smallest steps of progress. As we celebrate these wins, we honor the journey God has set before us, finding inspiration, motivation, and a deeper connection with His loving guidance.

CHAPTER FOUR
BUILDING RESILIENCE

Building Resilience

Building Resilience: Navigating Life's Challenges with Strength and Grace

Resilience is the remarkable capacity of individuals to bounce back from adversity, to withstand challenges and setbacks, and to emerge stronger, wiser, and more determined. It is a dynamic trait that empowers individuals to navigate life's storms with a sense of inner strength, adaptability, and grace. Building resilience involves cultivating a set of skills, attitudes, and strategies that allow individuals to not only survive difficult circumstances but also thrive in the face of them.

1. Positive Mindset

Building resilience begins with cultivating a positive mindset. This involves adopting an optimistic outlook, even in the midst of challenges. Philippians 4:8 (NIV) encourages, "Finally, brothers and sisters, whatever is true, whatever is noble, whatever is right, whatever is pure, whatever is lovely, whatever is admirable—if anything is excellent or praiseworthy—think about such things." Focusing on the positive aspects of a situation can help individuals build resilience by nurturing a hopeful and constructive perspective.

2. Adaptability and Flexibility

Resilience thrives on adaptability and flexibility. Proverbs 24:16 (NIV) teaches, "for though the righteous fall seven times, they rise again, but the wicked stumble when calamity strikes." Embracing change and uncertainty while maintaining a sense of purpose and determination allows individuals to adjust their approach and find new paths forward, even when faced with adversity.

3. Problem-Solving Skills

Building resilience involves honing problem-solving skills. James 1:5 (NIV) advises, "If any of you lacks wisdom, you should ask God, who gives generously to all without finding fault, and it will be given to you." Seeking guidance and developing effective problem-solving strategies can empower individuals to confront challenges head-on and find solutions that lead to growth and resolution.

4. Social Support

Strong social connections play a crucial role in resilience. Ecclesiastes 4:9-10 (NIV) emphasizes the strength in unity: "Two are better than one, because they have a good return for their labor: If either of them falls down, one can help the other up." Cultivating a network of supportive relationships provides emotional and practical assistance during difficult times, enhancing an individual's ability to cope and recover.

5. Self-Care and Wellness

Resilience is nurtured through self-care and wellness practices. 1 Corinthians 6:19-20 (NIV) reminds us, "Do you not know that your bodies are temples of the Holy Spirit, who is in you, whom you have received from God? You are not your own." Prioritizing physical, mental, and emotional well-being equips individuals with the energy and strength needed to face challenges with resilience and determination.

6. Acceptance of Imperfection

Resilience involves accepting imperfection and learning from failures. Romans 8:28 (NIV) assures, "And we know that in all things God works for the good of those who love him, who have been called according to his purpose." Embracing mistakes as opportunities for growth and seeing challenges as part of a larger purpose can help individuals build resilience by fostering a sense of purpose and meaning.

7. Faith and Spiritual Strength

Central to resilience is a foundation of faith and spiritual strength. Isaiah 41:10 (NIV) provides comfort and assurance: "So do not fear, for I am with you; do not be dismayed, for I am your God. I will strengthen you and help you; I will uphold you with my righteous right hand." Trusting in God's guidance and leaning on one's spiritual beliefs can provide a deep well of strength and resilience in times of difficulty.

Hence, building resilience is a transformative journey that combines practical skills with a firm foundation of faith, optimism, and adaptability. Through a positive mindset, problem-solving skills, social support, self-care, and a deep connection with one's spiritual beliefs, individuals can navigate life's challenges with grace and strength. Resilience not only allows us to overcome adversity but also empowers us to thrive, learn, and grow in the face of life's inevitable trials. By building resilience, we embrace the fullness of our human experience and draw upon our inner and spiritual resources to emerge from challenges stronger, wiser, and more capable than before.

Building Resilience: A Biblical Perspective on Strength Amidst Adversity

Building resilience is a transformative journey that aligns with profound biblical principles of perseverance, faith, and unwavering trust in God's guidance. Resilience empowers individuals to navigate life's challenges with grace, strength, and a steadfast spirit, allowing them to endure difficulties, bounce back from setbacks, and emerge stronger than before.

1. Biblical Foundation of Perseverance

Resilience is rooted in the biblical concept of perseverance. Romans 5:3-4 (NIV) states, "Not only so, but we also glory in our sufferings, because we know that suffering produces perseverance; perseverance, character; and character, hope." Building resilience involves enduring hardships with patience and determination, recognizing that challenges contribute to the development of character and a hopeful outlook.

2. Trusting in God's Strength

Isaiah 40:31 (NIV) offers a powerful assurance: "but those who hope in the Lord will renew their strength. They will soar on wings like eagles; they will run and not grow weary; they will walk and not be faint." Building resilience requires trusting in God's strength and leaning on Him for guidance. This trust empowers individuals to rise above adversity and face difficulties with a renewed spirit.

3. Embracing Adversity as Growth

James 1:2-4 (NIV) emphasizes the transformative nature of trials: "Consider it pure joy, my brothers and sisters, whenever you face trials of many kinds, because you know that the testing of your faith produces perseverance. Let perseverance finish its work so that you may be mature and complete, not lacking anything." Resilience involves embracing adversity as an opportunity for spiritual and personal growth, allowing perseverance to shape character and maturity.

4. Hope Amidst Challenges

Building resilience nurtures a sense of hope, even in challenging circumstances. Psalm 42:11 (NIV) imparts, "Why, my soul, are you downcast? Why so disturbed within me? Put your hope in God, for I will yet praise him, my Savior and my God." Resilience enables individuals to hold onto hope, finding solace in God's promises and maintaining a positive outlook, even when faced with trials.

5. Overcoming Fear and Anxiety

Resilience empowers individuals to overcome fear and anxiety. Philippians 4:6-7 (NIV) encourages, "Do not be anxious about anything, but in every situation, by prayer and petition, with thanksgiving, present your requests to God. And the peace of God, which transcends all understanding, will guard your hearts and your minds in Christ Jesus." By entrusting their concerns to God, resilient individuals find inner peace and strength to face challenges.

6. Restoration and Renewal

The process of building resilience is akin to restoration and renewal. Psalm 23:3 (NIV) affirms, "He refreshes my soul. He guides me along the right paths for his name's sake." Resilience involves allowing God to refresh and guide the soul through difficulties, leading to a sense of renewal and a deeper connection with one's faith.

7. Trusting God's Plan

Proverbs 3:5-6 (NIV) encapsulates the essence of building resilience: "Trust in the Lord with all your heart and lean not on your own understanding; in all your ways submit to him, and he will make your paths straight." Resilient individuals trust in God's plan, submitting their challenges and uncertainties to Him, confident that He will guide them toward a path of strength and purpose.

Hence, building resilience is a journey of faith, perseverance, and hope, deeply intertwined with biblical principles of endurance and trust in God's providence. By embracing challenges as opportunities for growth, leaning on God's strength, and maintaining a hopeful perspective, individuals can navigate life's trials with grace and emerge stronger, more mature, and spiritually enriched. Resilience empowers us to face adversity head-on, confident that God's steadfast love and guidance will carry us through every storm, enabling us to shine as beacons of strength and unwavering faith.

4.1 Understanding the nature of resilience

Understanding the Nature of Resilience: The Power to Thrive Amidst Adversity

Resilience is a multifaceted and dynamic trait that embodies the capacity of individuals to adapt, persevere, and thrive in the face of adversity. It is a fundamental quality that empowers us to overcome challenges, bounce back from setbacks, and navigate the complexities of life with strength, courage, and grace. To truly understand the nature of resilience, one must delve into its components, its psychological underpinnings, and its profound impact on personal growth and well-being.

1. Adaptive Response to Adversity

At its core, resilience is an adaptive response to adversity. It is the ability to confront difficulties, setbacks, and hardships with a mindset geared towards growth and transformation. Resilient individuals do not merely endure challenges; they harness them as opportunities for learning, self-discovery, and positive change. This mirrors the biblical principle found in Romans 8:28 (NIV): "And we know that in all things God works for the good of those who love him, who have been called according to his purpose." Resilience enables us to trust that even in trials, there is a greater purpose unfolding.

2. Psychological Strength and Flexibility

Resilience involves psychological strength and flexibility. It encompasses the capacity to manage emotions, maintain perspective, and adapt one's mindset to navigate varying circumstances. Just as 2 Corinthians 12:9 (NIV) reminds us, "My grace is sufficient for you, for my power is made perfect in weakness," resilience allows us to draw upon inner strength and rely on God's grace to guide us through moments of vulnerability.

3. Coping Strategies and Resources

Resilience is not a passive trait; it involves active coping strategies and the utilization of personal and external resources. Individuals who are resilient often tap into a support network, seek guidance, and engage in self-care practices to bolster their ability to manage challenges. Proverbs 11:14 (NIV) underscores the importance of counsel: "For lack of guidance a nation falls, but victory is won through many advisers." Resilience acknowledges the value of seeking wise counsel in times of need.

4. Growth and Transformation

Resilience is intertwined with the concept of growth and transformation. It allows individuals to evolve and expand beyond their comfort zones. Just as 2 Corinthians 3:18 (NIV) expresses, "And we all, who with unveiled faces contemplate the Lord's glory, are being transformed into his image with ever-increasing glory," resilience enables us to embrace challenges as opportunities for spiritual and personal refinement.

5. Empowerment and Self-Efficacy

Resilience empowers individuals by enhancing their sense of self-efficacy—the belief in their ability to overcome obstacles. This aligns with Philippians 4:13 (NIV): "I can do all this through him who gives me strength." Resilient individuals acknowledge their strengths and their connection with a higher power, enabling them to face challenges with unwavering confidence.

6. Coping with Uncertainty

In a world marked by uncertainty, resilience equips individuals with the tools to cope and adapt. Psalm 62:5 (NIV) reassures, "Yes, my soul, find rest in God; my hope comes from him." Resilience fosters a sense of inner rest and hope, allowing individuals to navigate the unknown with a calm and steady spirit.

7. Building Meaningful Relationships

Resilience is closely tied to the cultivation of meaningful relationships. Ecclesiastes 4:12 (NIV) illustrates the strength in unity: "Though one may be overpowered, two can defend themselves. A cord of three strands is not quickly broken." Resilient individuals often draw strength from their relationships, recognizing that support and connection contribute to their ability to withstand challenges.

Therefore, understanding the nature of resilience reveals its profound impact on our lives—shaping our responses to adversity, nurturing personal growth, and deepening our spiritual connection. Resilience is a journey of adapting, learning, and transforming, guided by principles of faith, inner strength, and resourcefulness. Just as a tree withstands storms and continues to grow, resilience empowers us to stand firm in the face of life's challenges, emerge from difficulties with newfound wisdom, and continue our journey with an unwavering spirit of hope and determination.

Understanding the Nature of Resilience: *A Biblical Perspective on Strength and Endurance:*

Resilience is a profound quality that embodies the ability to withstand adversity, bounce back from setbacks, and thrive despite life's challenges. Rooted in biblical principles, resilience is a testament to the strength, endurance, and unwavering faith of individuals as they navigate the complexities of life.

1. Endurance Through Trials

Resilience is closely aligned with endurance through trials. James 1:12 (NIV) states, "Blessed is the one who perseveres under trial because, having stood the test, that person will receive the crown of life that the Lord has promised to those who love him." Resilient individuals understand that trials are opportunities for growth and refinement, and they endure with hope for the promised rewards.

2. Trusting in God's Plan

Proverbs 3:5-6 (NIV) guides the nature of resilience: "Trust in the Lord with all your heart and lean not on your own understanding; in all your ways submit to him, and he will make your paths straight." Resilience is rooted in trusting God's divine plan, even when circumstances seem challenging or confusing. By submitting to His guidance, individuals find strength to overcome obstacles.

3. Perseverance Through Hardships

Romans 5:3-4 (NIV) illustrates the role of resilience in perseverance: "Not only so, but we also glory in our sufferings, because we know that suffering produces perseverance; perseverance, character; and character, hope." Resilience is the bridge that leads from suffering to character development and a hopeful outlook. Enduring through hardships builds character and strengthens one's ability to face future challenges.

4. Joy in Tribulations

Resilience enables individuals to find joy amidst tribulations. Romans 12:12 (NIV) encourages, "Be joyful in hope, patient in affliction, faithful in prayer." This perspective allows resilient individuals to maintain a positive attitude even when facing difficulties, focusing on the hope that sustains them through the storm.

5. Strength in Weakness

2 Corinthians 12:9-10 (NIV) speaks to the paradox of strength in weakness: "But he said to me, 'My grace is sufficient for you, for my power is made perfect in weakness.' Therefore, I will boast all the more gladly about my weaknesses, so that Christ's power may rest on me. That is why, for Christ's sake, I delight in weaknesses, in insults, in hardships, in persecutions, in difficulties. For when I am weak, then I am strong." Resilience acknowledges human vulnerability and embraces God's strength in times of weakness, allowing His power to shine through.

6. Renewed Strength

Isaiah 40:31 (NIV) captures the essence of resilience: "But those who hope in the Lord will renew their strength. They will soar on wings like eagles; they will run and not grow weary; they will walk and not be faint." Resilience is the embodiment of hope in God's promises, leading to renewed strength that enables individuals to rise above challenges and continue their journey.

7. A Solid Foundation

Matthew 7:24-25 (NIV) illustrates the importance of a solid foundation: "Therefore everyone who hears these words of mine and puts them into practice is like a wise man who built his house on the rock. The rain came down, the streams rose, and the winds blew and beat against that house; yet it did not fall, because it had its foundation on the rock." Resilience is built on the foundation of faith and obedience to God's teachings, providing stability and strength during life's storms.

Understanding the nature of resilience reveals its profound connection to biblical principles of endurance, trust, and unwavering faith. Resilience enables individuals to endure trials, trust in God's plan, persevere through hardships, find joy amidst tribulations, draw strength from weakness, experience renewal, and establish a solid foundation. Just as a tree's roots anchor it during storms, resilience anchors us in God's promises, empowering us to navigate life's challenges with courage, hope, and a steadfast spirit.

4.2 Developing emotional intelligence

Developing Emotional Intelligence: Nurturing the Power of Self-Awareness and Empathy

Emotional intelligence (EI) is the ability to recognize, understand, and manage one's own emotions while also effectively perceiving and responding to the emotions of others. It is a critical skill that plays a central role in personal relationships, social interactions, and overall well-being. Developing emotional intelligence involves cultivating self-awareness, empathy, interpersonal skills, and emotional regulation, leading to healthier relationships and greater emotional resilience.

1. Self-Awareness

At the heart of emotional intelligence lies self-awareness—a deep understanding of one's own emotions, strengths, weaknesses, and triggers. Proverbs 20:27 (NIV) reflects this principle: "The human spirit is the lamp of the Lord that sheds light on one's inmost being." Developing emotional intelligence begins with introspection, allowing individuals to shed light on their inner thoughts and feelings. By recognizing their emotional responses, they can navigate situations with greater clarity and mindfulness.

2. Empathy

Empathy is the ability to recognize and share the feelings of others. Romans 12:15 (NIV) captures the essence of empathy: "Rejoice with those who rejoice; mourn with those who mourn." Developing emotional intelligence includes stepping into others' shoes, actively listening, and seeking to understand their perspectives. Cultivating empathy fosters deeper connections and builds bridges of understanding in relationships.

3. Effective Communication

Emotional intelligence enhances communication skills, both verbal and nonverbal. Proverbs 15:1 (NIV) emphasizes the impact of words: "A gentle answer turns away wrath, but a harsh word stirs up anger." Developing emotional intelligence allows individuals to express themselves effectively, using words and gestures that foster positive interactions and prevent misunderstandings.

4. Emotional Regulation

Emotional intelligence involves regulating one's own emotions and managing impulsive reactions. James 1:19-20 (NIV) provides guidance: "My dear brothers and sisters, take note of this: Everyone should be quick to listen, slow to speak and slow to become angry, because human anger does not produce the righteousness that God desires." Developing emotional intelligence enables individuals to control emotional outbursts and respond thoughtfully, aligning with God's desire for righteous behavior.

5. Conflict Resolution

Developing emotional intelligence contributes to effective conflict resolution. Matthew 5:9 (NIV) emphasizes peacemaking: "Blessed are the peacemakers, for they will be called children of God." Emotionally intelligent individuals navigate conflicts with empathy and understanding, striving for resolutions that promote harmony and reconciliation.

6. Social Awareness

Social awareness is a key element of emotional intelligence, involving the ability to recognize and navigate social dynamics. Proverbs 22:24-25 (NIV) offers counsel on choosing companions: "Do not make friends with a hot-tempered person, do not associate with one easily angered." Developing emotional intelligence empowers individuals to discern healthy relationships and respond appropriately to diverse social situations.

7. Cultivating Resilience

Emotionally intelligent individuals often exhibit greater resilience in the face of challenges. Psalm 23:4 (NIV) offers comfort in difficult times: "Even though I walk through the darkest valley, I will fear no evil, for you are with me." Developing emotional intelligence equips individuals to navigate adversity with a balanced perspective, drawing on their emotional awareness to find inner strength and peace.

Developing emotional intelligence is a transformative journey that aligns with biblical principles of self-awareness, empathy, effective communication, emotional regulation, conflict resolution, social awareness, and resilience. By honing these skills, individuals enhance their relationships, promote understanding, and navigate life's complexities with grace and wisdom. Just as Jesus exemplified compassion and understanding, developing emotional intelligence empowers individuals to connect more deeply with themselves and others, fostering a world marked by empathy, compassion, and authentic connections.

Developing Emotional Intelligence: A Biblical Guide to Understanding and Nurturing Our Emotions

Emotional intelligence (EI) is a transformative concept rooted in biblical wisdom that revolves around recognizing, understanding, and effectively managing our own emotions while also empathizing and responding to the emotions of others. Through the lens of scripture, we can explore the development of emotional intelligence as a path to better relationships, enhanced self-awareness, and a deeper connection with God.

1. Self-Awareness

Proverbs 4:23 (NIV) guides us to guard our hearts, for "everything you do flows from it." Developing emotional intelligence begins with self-awareness, acknowledging and understanding our emotions as the wellspring of our actions. Just as the psalmist implores in Psalm 139:23-24 (NIV), "Search me, God, and know my heart; test me and know my anxious thoughts. See if there is any offensive way in me, and lead me in the way everlasting." Reflecting on our emotions and seeking divine insight helps us navigate our inner landscape.

2. Empathy

Empathy, a cornerstone of emotional intelligence, resonates with Jesus' teachings about loving our neighbors as ourselves. Matthew 22:39 (NIV) instructs us, "And the second is like it: 'Love your neighbor as yourself.'" By putting ourselves in others' shoes, we embrace empathy, just as Ephesians 4:32 (NIV) encourages us to "be kind and compassionate to one another, forgiving each other, just as in Christ God forgave you."

3. Self-Control and Patience

Developing emotional intelligence involves self-control and patience. Proverbs 16:32 (NIV) states, "Better a patient person than a warrior, one with self-control than one who takes a city." Emotional intelligence empowers us to manage our emotions, responding with patience and self-control, echoing Galatians 5:22-23 (NIV): "But the fruit of the Spirit is love, joy, peace, forbearance, kindness, goodness, faithfulness, gentleness and self-control."

4. Communication

Effective communication is a vital component of emotional intelligence. Proverbs 15:1 (NIV) illustrates this: "A gentle answer turns away wrath, but a harsh word stirs up anger." James 1:19 (NIV) further advises, "My dear brothers and sisters, take note of this: Everyone should be quick to listen, slow to speak and slow to become angry." Developing emotional intelligence allows us to communicate with humility and understanding.

5. Compassion and Healing

Emotional intelligence leads to compassion and healing, mirroring Jesus' ministry. Matthew 14:14 (NIV) recounts, "When Jesus landed and saw a large crowd, he had compassion on them and healed their sick." Developing empathy and compassion enables us to extend healing to emotional wounds, fulfilling the mandate to bear one another's burdens (Galatians 6:2, NIV).

6. Conflict Resolution

Emotional intelligence aids in conflict resolution. Proverbs 20:3 (NIV) advises, "It is to one's honor to avoid strife, but every fool is quick to quarrel." The development of emotional intelligence empowers us to navigate conflicts with humility and grace, seeking resolution in the spirit of love and understanding.

7. Joy and Resilience

Developing emotional intelligence can lead to greater joy and resilience. Nehemiah 8:10 (NIV) affirms, "The joy of the Lord is your strength." By understanding and managing our emotions, we enhance our capacity to find joy and maintain resilience even in the face of challenges, as Paul attests in Philippians 4:12-13 (NIV).

Conclusion

Developing emotional intelligence is a transformative journey guided by biblical principles of self-awareness, empathy, self-control, effective communication, compassion, conflict resolution, joy, and resilience. As we align our emotional growth with God's word, we cultivate deeper connections, healthier relationships, and a more authentic expression of our faith. Emotional intelligence becomes a tool for embodying the love and compassion that Jesus exemplified, fostering a world marked by understanding, grace, and emotional well-being.

4.3 Strategies to bounce back from setbacks

Bouncing Back from Setbacks: Strategies for Resilience and Growth

Setbacks are an inevitable part of life's journey, challenging us to navigate adversity and emerge stronger than before. Developing effective strategies to bounce back from setbacks is a crucial skill that empowers us to transform challenges into opportunities for growth, build resilience, and continue pursuing our goals with renewed determination. These strategies encompass a blend of psychological, emotional, and practical approaches, guided by biblical principles and wisdom.

1. Resilient Mindset

Cultivating a resilient mindset is foundational to bouncing back from setbacks. Romans 12:12 (NIV) encourages us to be "joyful in hope, patient in affliction, faithful in prayer." Embracing hope, patience, and faith through prayer empowers us to view setbacks as temporary hurdles, fostering the belief that challenges are surmountable and that better days lie ahead.

2. Acceptance and Self-Compassion

Accepting setbacks with self-compassion is key to the healing process. Proverbs 19:11 (NIV) underscores the importance of patience and self-control: "A person's wisdom yields patience; it is to one's glory to overlook an offense." Rather than dwelling on self-blame or criticism, practicing self-compassion acknowledges that setbacks are a part of the human experience, leading to greater emotional resilience.

3. Learn and Adapt

Setbacks provide invaluable lessons. James 1:3-4 (NIV) reveals that trials produce perseverance and maturity: "because you know that the testing of your faith produces perseverance. Let perseverance finish its work so that you may be mature and complete, not lacking anything." Evaluating setbacks for the lessons they offer enables us to make informed decisions, adapt our strategies, and grow in wisdom.

4. Seek Support

Isolation in times of setback can intensify the impact. Ecclesiastes 4:9-10 (NIV) highlights the strength of companionship: "Two are better than one, because they have a good return for their labor: If either of them falls down, one can help the other up." Seeking emotional support from friends, family, or a mentor provides comfort, perspective, and guidance during challenging times.

5. Set Realistic Goals

Setbacks may require reevaluating goals and setting realistic expectations. Proverbs 16:3 (NIV) reminds us to commit our plans to the Lord: "Commit to the Lord whatever you do, and he will establish your plans." Seeking divine guidance while adjusting our goals allows us to move forward with purpose and clarity.

6. Positive Affirmations

Positive affirmations align with biblical principles of faith and hope. Philippians 4:13 (NIV) states, "I can do all this through him who gives me strength." Repeating affirmations that resonate with our faith reinforces a positive outlook, enhancing our resilience and encouraging us to persevere through setbacks.

7. Take Action and Persevere

Taking deliberate action in the face of setbacks is essential. James 2:26 (NIV) emphasizes faith combined with action: "As the body without the spirit is dead, so faith without deeds is dead." While setbacks may present challenges, taking consistent steps forward—no matter how small—builds momentum and fosters a sense of accomplishment.

8. Practice Gratitude

Gratitude shifts our focus from setbacks to the blessings present in our lives. 1 Thessalonians 5:18 (NIV) directs us to "give thanks in all circumstances; for this is God's will for you in Christ Jesus." Cultivating gratitude helps us maintain a positive perspective, promoting emotional well-being and resilience.

Conclusion

Strategies to bounce back from setbacks blend psychological insights with timeless biblical wisdom. By embracing a resilient mindset, practicing self-compassion, learning from setbacks, seeking support, setting realistic goals, affirming faith, taking action, and cultivating gratitude, we empower ourselves to transform setbacks into stepping stones. Just as setbacks are a part of our journey, so too is the capacity to rise above them, drawing strength from God's guidance, our inner resources, and the support of our community. Through these strategies, setbacks become opportunities for growth, resilience, and a deeper connection to our purpose.

Strategies to Bounce Back from Setbacks: A Biblical Approach to Overcoming Adversity

Life is marked by setbacks—challenges that test our resolve, resilience, and faith. However, setbacks need not define us; they can become catalysts for growth and transformation. Through a blend of practical strategies and timeless biblical wisdom, we can navigate setbacks with grace, courage, and the assurance that God's guidance is ever-present.

1. Resilient Faith and Hope

Developing a resilient faith and nurturing hope are foundational strategies to bounce back from setbacks. Romans 15:13 (NIV) assures us, "May the God of hope fill you with all joy and peace as you trust in him, so that you may overflow with hope by the power of the Holy Spirit." Anchoring ourselves in God's promises and maintaining hope during setbacks fosters a positive outlook and provides strength to endure.

2. Learning from Trials

James 1:2-4 (NIV) imparts wisdom about the role of trials: "Consider it pure joy, my brothers and sisters, whenever you face trials of many kinds, because you know that the testing of your faith produces perseverance. Let perseverance finish its work so that you may be mature and complete, not lacking anything." Embracing setbacks as opportunities for growth and character development positions us to learn from adversity and emerge stronger.

3. Relying on God's Strength

In times of setbacks, relying on our own strength may prove inadequate. 2 Corinthians 12:9 (NIV) reminds us of the sufficiency of God's grace: "My grace is sufficient for you, for my power is made perfect in weakness." Recognizing our dependence on God's strength empowers us to overcome setbacks with humility and trust.

4. Seeking Wisdom and Guidance

Proverbs 3:5-6 (NIV) underscores the importance of seeking divine guidance: "Trust in the Lord with all your heart and lean not on your own understanding; in all your ways submit to him, and he will make your paths straight." When facing setbacks, seeking God's wisdom and guidance through prayer and reflection can illuminate a clear path forward.

5. Persistence and Perseverance

Setbacks require persistence and perseverance. Galatians 6:9 (NIV) encourages us, "Let us not become weary in doing good, for at the proper time we will reap a harvest if we do not give up." Persevering through setbacks, even when challenges seem insurmountable, can lead to eventual breakthroughs and rewards.

6. Embracing God's Timing

Ecclesiastes 3:1 (NIV) reminds us, "There is a time for everything, and a season for every activity under the heavens." Bouncing back from setbacks involves acknowledging that setbacks are part of life's seasons. Trusting in God's timing and purpose allows us to approach setbacks with patience and a sense of divine order.

7. Cultivating Gratitude

Practicing gratitude amid setbacks helps shift our focus from challenges to blessings. 1 Thessalonians 5:18 (NIV) instructs us, "give thanks in all circumstances; for this is God's will for you in Christ Jesus." Expressing gratitude for the lessons learned, the support received, and the growth experienced helps us maintain a positive perspective.

8. Turning Setbacks into Service

Bouncing back from setbacks can inspire us to serve others who face similar challenges. 2 Corinthians 1:3-4 (NIV) highlights this principle: "Praise be to the God and Father of our Lord Jesus Christ, the Father of compassion and the God of all comfort, who comforts us in all our troubles, so that we can comfort those in any trouble with the comfort we ourselves receive from God." By sharing our experiences and offering comfort, setbacks can become opportunities to make a positive impact.

Bouncing back from setbacks requires a harmonious blend of practical strategies and biblical principles. By nurturing a resilient faith, learning from trials, relying on God's strength, seeking divine guidance, practicing perseverance, embracing God's timing, cultivating gratitude, and turning setbacks into service, we can navigate adversity with a sense of purpose and resilience. Through these strategies, setbacks become stepping stones, leading us toward a deeper understanding of ourselves, a stronger connection with God, and a more profound impact on the world around us.

4.4 The role of self-care in building resilience

Strategies to Bounce Back from Setbacks: A Biblical Approach to Overcoming Adversity

Life is marked by setbacks—challenges that test our resolve, resilience, and faith. However, setbacks need not define us; they can become catalysts for growth and transformation. Through a blend of practical strategies and timeless biblical wisdom, we can navigate setbacks with grace, courage, and the assurance that God's guidance is ever-present.

1. Resilient Faith and Hope

Developing a resilient faith and nurturing hope are foundational strategies to bounce back from setbacks. Romans 15:13 (NIV) assures us, "May the God of hope fill you with all joy and peace as you trust in him, so that you may overflow with hope by the power of the Holy Spirit." Anchoring ourselves in God's promises and maintaining hope during setbacks fosters a positive outlook and provides strength to endure.

2. Learning from Trials

James 1:2-4 (NIV) imparts wisdom about the role of trials: "Consider it pure joy, my brothers and sisters, whenever you face trials of many kinds, because you know that the testing of your faith produces perseverance. Let perseverance finish its work so that you may be mature and complete, not lacking anything." Embracing setbacks as opportunities for growth and character development positions us to learn from adversity and emerge stronger.

3. Relying on God's Strength

In times of setbacks, relying on our own strength may prove inadequate. 2 Corinthians 12:9 (NIV) reminds us of the sufficiency of

God's grace: "My grace is sufficient for you, for my power is made perfect in weakness." Recognizing our dependence on God's strength empowers us to overcome setbacks with humility and trust.

4. Seeking Wisdom and Guidance

Proverbs 3:5-6 (NIV) underscores the importance of seeking divine guidance: "Trust in the Lord with all your heart and lean not on your own understanding; in all your ways submit to him, and he will make your paths straight." When facing setbacks, seeking God's wisdom and guidance through prayer and reflection can illuminate a clear path forward.

5. Persistence and Perseverance

Setbacks require persistence and perseverance. Galatians 6:9 (NIV) encourages us, "Let us not become weary in doing good, for at the proper time we will reap a harvest if we do not give up." Persevering through setbacks, even when challenges seem insurmountable, can lead to eventual breakthroughs and rewards.

6. Embracing God's Timing

Ecclesiastes 3:1 (NIV) reminds us, "There is a time for everything, and a season for every activity under the heavens." Bouncing back from setbacks involves acknowledging that setbacks are part of life's seasons. Trusting in God's timing and purpose allows us to approach setbacks with patience and a sense of divine order.

7. Cultivating Gratitude

Practicing gratitude amid setbacks helps shift our focus from challenges to blessings. 1 Thessalonians 5:18 (NIV) instructs us, "give thanks in all circumstances; for this is God's will for you in Christ Jesus." Expressing gratitude for the lessons learned, the support received, and the growth experienced helps us maintain a positive perspective.

8. Turning Setbacks into Service

Bouncing back from setbacks can inspire us to serve others who face similar challenges. 2 Corinthians 1:3-4 (NIV) highlights this principle: "Praise be to the God and Father of our Lord Jesus Christ, the Father of compassion and the God of all comfort, who comforts us in all our troubles, so that we can comfort those in any trouble with the comfort we ourselves receive from God." By sharing our experiences and offering comfort, setbacks can become opportunities to make a positive impact.

Conclusion

Bouncing back from setbacks requires a harmonious blend of practical strategies and biblical principles. By nurturing a resilient faith, learning from trials, relying on God's strength, seeking divine guidance, practicing perseverance, embracing God's timing, cultivating gratitude, and turning setbacks into service, we can navigate adversity with a sense of purpose and resilience. Through these strategies, setbacks become stepping stones, leading us toward a deeper understanding of ourselves, a stronger connection with God, and a more profound impact on the world around us.

The Role of Self-Care in Building Resilience: Nurturing Strength Amidst Life's Challenges

Resilience, the ability to bounce back from adversity and thrive despite setbacks, is a quality that empowers individuals to navigate life's storms with grace and determination. One vital cornerstone of resilience is self-care—an intentional and holistic practice that encompasses nurturing one's physical, mental, emotional, and spiritual well-being. By prioritizing self-care, individuals build a solid foundation of strength and endurance, equipping themselves to face challenges with resilience and emerge from difficult experiences stronger than before.

1. Physical Well-Being

Caring for one's physical health is a crucial aspect of building resilience. Our bodies and minds are interconnected, and a healthy body provides the energy and vitality needed to overcome challenges. Adequate sleep, regular exercise, and a balanced diet contribute to physical well-being, supporting the body's ability to cope with stress. 1 Corinthians 6:19-20 (NIV) reminds us that our bodies are temples of the Holy Spirit, urging us to honor and care for them.

2. Mental and Emotional Health

Self-care extends to mental and emotional health, nurturing a resilient mindset. Philippians 4:8 (NIV) guides us: "Finally, brothers and sisters, whatever is true, whatever is noble, whatever is right, whatever is pure, whatever is lovely, whatever is admirable—if anything is excellent or praiseworthy—think about such things." Engaging in mindfulness, practicing gratitude, and seeking professional support when needed contribute to mental and emotional well-being, enhancing one's ability to cope with adversity.

3. Stress Management

Effective stress management is a key element of self-care and resilience. Psalm 55:22 (NIV) offers solace: "Cast your cares on the

Lord and he will sustain you; he will never let the righteous be shaken." Engaging in relaxation techniques, such as deep breathing, meditation, and spending time in nature, helps individuals manage stress and maintain emotional equilibrium.

4. Boundaries and Saying No

Setting boundaries and knowing when to say no are vital self-care practices. Jesus himself demonstrated the importance of boundaries by withdrawing to solitary places for prayer (Luke 5:16, NIV). By honoring one's limits and making space for rest and rejuvenation, individuals preserve their energy and emotional reserves, enhancing their capacity to face challenges with resilience.

5. Nurturing Relationships

Healthy relationships are a source of strength and support. Proverbs 17:17 (NIV) emphasizes the value of a friend's love: "A friend loves at all times, and a brother is born for a time of adversity." Prioritizing time with loved ones, cultivating a strong support network, and seeking emotional connection contribute to emotional resilience.

6. Pursuing Passions

Engaging in activities that bring joy and fulfillment is an integral aspect of self-care. Ecclesiastes 3:13 (NIV) acknowledges the enjoyment of life's gifts: "That each of them may eat and drink, and find satisfaction in all their toil—this is the gift of God." Pursuing passions and hobbies rejuvenates the spirit, fosters creativity, and provides a sense of purpose beyond challenges.

7. Rest and Renewal

Rest is a divine prescription for renewal. Psalm 23:2-3 (NIV) illustrates God's provision: "He makes me lie down in green pastures, he leads me beside quiet waters, he refreshes my soul." Intentionally carving out time for rest, Sabbath, and moments of reflection replenishes the spirit and equips individuals to face challenges with a clear and rejuvenated perspective.

Conclusion

Self-care is an indispensable pillar of building resilience. By nurturing physical well-being, tending to mental and emotional health, managing stress, setting boundaries, fostering relationships, pursuing passions, and prioritizing rest, individuals create a strong foundation for resilience. Just as a well-tended garden flourishes despite changing weather, practicing self-care nurtures inner strength and equips individuals to weather life's storms while maintaining a steadfast and resilient spirit. In the tapestry of life's challenges and triumphs, self-care threads a resilient narrative of endurance, growth, and well-being.

CHAPTER FIVE
CONQUERING THE FEAR OF
JUDGMENT

Conquering the Fear of Judgment

Conquering the Fear of Judgment: Liberating Yourself from the Chains of Others' Opinions

The fear of judgment, a potent and universal human emotion, has the power to hinder personal growth, stifle self-expression, and hinder one's pursuit of purpose. This fear, rooted in the concern for how others perceive us, often leads to self-doubt, anxiety, and an unfulfilled life. Conquering the fear of judgment is a transformative journey that liberates individuals from the constraints of external opinions, empowers them to embrace authenticity, and fosters a sense of freedom and self-empowerment.

1. Recognizing the Source of Fear

Conquering the fear of judgment begins with acknowledging its source. Matthew 10:28 (NIV) offers perspective: "Do not be afraid of those who kill the body but cannot kill the soul. Rather, be afraid of the One who can destroy both soul and body in hell." Realizing that the opinions of others hold no eternal significance helps diminish the power of external judgment.

2. Embracing Self-Acceptance

Accepting oneself fully is a powerful antidote to the fear of judgment. Psalm 139:14 (NIV) reminds us of our inherent worth: "I praise you because I am fearfully and wonderfully made; your works are wonderful; I know that full well." When individuals embrace their unique qualities and understand that they are created intentionally by God, the fear of external judgment loses its grip.

3. Shifting Focus Inward

Redirecting focus from external validation to inner fulfillment is pivotal. Galatians 1:10 (NIV) encourages seeking God's approval above all else: "Am I now trying to win the approval of human beings, or of God? Or am I trying to please people? If I were still trying to please people, I would not be a servant of Christ." By aligning actions with God's will and purpose, the fear of judgment fades as individuals prioritizes divine affirmation.

4. Practicing Authenticity

Choosing authenticity over conformity is a liberating step. Romans 12:2 (NIV) emphasizes transformation through renewing the mind: "Do not conform to the pattern of this world, but be transformed by the renewing of your mind. Then you will be able to test and approve what God's will is—his good, pleasing and perfect will." By living authentically and in accordance with God's will, individuals break free from the fear of societal norms and expectations.

5. Embracing Vulnerability

Embracing vulnerability fosters emotional resilience. 2 Corinthians 12:9 (NIV) illustrates strength in weakness: "But he said to me, 'My grace is sufficient for you, for my power is made perfect in weakness.' Therefore, I will boast all the more gladly about my weaknesses, so that Christ's power may rest on me." When individuals share their struggles and vulnerabilities, they discover a deep connection with others and find that authenticity is a powerful testimony.

6. Focusing on Contribution

Shifting focus from self-concern to contributing positively to the world lessens the fear of judgment. 1 Peter 4:10 (NIV) highlights using God-given gifts to serve others: "Each of you should use whatever gift you have received to serve others, as faithful stewards of God's grace in its various forms." By channeling energy into making a positive impact, individuals transcend their own insecurities and find purpose beyond the fear of judgment.

7. Seeking Support and Encouragement

Surrounding oneself with a supportive community provides strength. Ecclesiastes 4:9-10 (NIV) speaks of companionship: "Two are better than one, because they have a good return for their labor: If either of them falls down, one can help the other up." Connecting with like-minded individuals who uplift and encourage each other counteracts the isolating effects of the fear of judgment.

Conclusion

Conquering the fear of judgment is a transformative journey that involves recognizing its source, embracing self-acceptance, shifting focus inward, practicing authenticity, embracing vulnerability, focusing on contribution, and seeking support. By anchoring one's identity in God's unconditional love and purpose, individuals liberate themselves from the chains of external opinions. In this liberation, they discover a newfound sense of freedom, authenticity, and empowerment, allowing them to fully embrace their God-given potential and live a life marked by courage, purpose, and unwavering faith.

Conquering the Fear of Judgment: Finding Liberation and Strength in Biblical Truth

The fear of judgment is a powerful emotion that often holds us captive, preventing us from living authentically and pursuing our true purpose. This fear, rooted in the worry of how others perceive us, can hinder our growth, self-expression, and the fulfillment of God's plan for our lives. However, the Bible offers profound wisdom and guidance on how to conquer this fear, enabling us to break free from its grip and live with confidence, authenticity, and a deep sense of purpose.

1. Recognizing God's Sovereignty

Matthew 10:28 (NIV) provides a perspective that shifts our focus from human opinions to God's authority: "Do not be afraid of those who kill the body but cannot kill the soul. Rather, be afraid of the One who can destroy both soul and body in hell." Recognizing that God's judgment is the ultimate truth helps us detach from the opinions of others and prioritize God's approval above all else.

2. Embracing Our Identity in Christ

1 John 4:18 (NIV) speaks to the power of God's love in dispelling fear: "There is no fear in love. But perfect love drives out fear, because fear has to do with punishment. The one who fears is not made perfect in love." By embracing our identity as beloved children of

God, we find security in His unconditional love, diminishing the impact of external judgments.

3. Seeking Divine Approval

Galatians 1:10 (NIV) encourages us to seek God's approval over human validation: "Am I now trying to win the approval of human beings, or of God? Or am I trying to please people? If I were still trying to please people, I would not be a servant of Christ." By aligning our actions with God's will and seeking His approval, we find a higher purpose that transcends the fear of human judgment.

4. Trusting in God's Design

Psalm 139:14 (NIV) reminds us of our unique creation by God: "I praise you because I am fearfully and wonderfully made; your works are wonderful; I know that full well." Trusting that God has intricately designed us for His purpose and delight empowers us to confidently embrace our authentic selves, regardless of external opinions.

5. Focusing on Eternal Values

Colossians 3:23-24 (NIV) emphasizes the significance of living for eternal rewards: "Whatever you do, work at it with all your heart, as working for the Lord, not for human masters, since you know that you will receive an inheritance from the Lord as a reward." When our focus shifts from seeking approval from people to seeking eternal rewards from God, the fear of judgment loses its power.

6. Overcoming with Love

1 Peter 4:8 (NIV) highlights the importance of love in overcoming fear: "Above all, love each other deeply, because love covers over a multitude of sins." By cultivating a heart of love—both for ourselves and others—we create an environment of grace and acceptance that diminishes the weight of judgment.

7. Finding Community and Encouragement

Hebrews 10:24-25 (NIV) underscores the value of community: "And let us consider how we may spur one another on toward love and good deeds, not giving up meeting together, as some are in the habit of doing, but encouraging one another—and all the more as you see the Day approaching." Surrounding ourselves with a supportive community helps us face judgment with resilience and encouragement.

Conclusion

Conquering the fear of judgment is a transformative process rooted in the wisdom of Scripture. By recognizing God's sovereignty, embracing our identity in Christ, seeking divine approval, trusting in God's design, focusing on eternal values, overcoming with love, and finding support in a community of believers, we can break free from the chains of fear. Through the power of God's truth and love, we discover the strength to live authentically, pursue our purpose boldly, and navigate life's challenges with unwavering faith and confidence.

5.1 Recognizing the fear of judgment and its impact

Recognizing the Fear of Judgment and Its Profound Impact: Unveiling the Chains that Hinder Growth

The fear of judgment is a deeply ingrained human emotion that exerts a powerful influence on our thoughts, actions, and decisions. Stemming from a natural desire for acceptance and belonging, this fear arises when we anticipate negative evaluations or criticism from others. While this fear is a normal aspect of human psychology, its impact can be far-reaching, affecting our self-esteem, relationships, and overall well-being. Recognizing the fear of judgment and understanding its implications is a crucial step toward breaking its hold and fostering personal growth.

1. Self-Censorship and Suppression

One of the most significant impacts of the fear of judgment is the tendency to censor oneself and suppress authentic thoughts and feelings. Fear of being perceived negatively can lead individuals to withhold their true opinions, ideas, and creativity. This self-censorship stifles self-expression and hampers personal growth, preventing individuals from fully embracing their uniqueness and contributing their authentic selves to the world.

2. Diminished Self-Esteem

The fear of judgment can erode self-esteem and self-worth. Constant worry about how others perceive us can lead to a cycle of negative self-talk and self-doubt. This, in turn, can hinder our ability to set and achieve goals, as well as to pursue new experiences or take calculated risks. Over time, the fear of judgment can create a pervasive sense of inadequacy and undermine our confidence in various aspects of life.

3. Strained Relationships

The fear of judgment can strain relationships by influencing our behavior and communication. In an attempt to avoid criticism or rejection, individuals may alter their actions or opinions to align with others' expectations. This can result in inauthentic interactions and a lack of genuine connection. Moreover, the constant fear of being judged can lead to overthinking, defensiveness, and difficulty in establishing trust within relationships.

4. Missed Opportunities

Many opportunities for personal and professional growth are often missed due to the fear of judgment. A reluctance to step outside one's comfort zone or take calculated risks can lead to stagnation and a limited scope of experiences. The fear of failure or disapproval may prevent individuals from pursuing new career paths, developing new skills, or seizing opportunities that could lead to self-discovery and success.

5. Unfulfilled Potential

Perhaps the most profound impact of the fear of judgment is its potential to hinder the realization of one's full potential. Jeremiah 1:5 (NIV) reminds us of God's divine purpose: "Before I formed you in the womb I knew you, before you were born, I set you apart." Each individual is uniquely designed with talents, passions, and a purpose to fulfill. Allowing the fear of judgment to dictate choices can rob individuals of the opportunity to fulfill God's intended plan for their lives.

6. Emotional Toll

The fear of judgment can exact a heavy emotional toll. Constant anxiety about others' opinions can lead to stress, anxiety disorders, and even depression. This emotional burden can diminish overall well-being, affecting both mental and physical health.

7. Hindrance to Spiritual Growth

The fear of judgment can also hinder spiritual growth. Instead of seeking God's approval, individuals may prioritize human validation, leading to a misalignment with God's purpose. Galatians 1:10 (NIV) emphasizes the importance of God's approval over human validation: "Am I now trying to win the approval of human beings, or of God? Or am I trying to please people? If I were still trying to please people, I would not be a servant of Christ."

Conclusion

The fear of judgment, though a common and natural human emotion, carries profound implications for personal growth, self-esteem, relationships, and spiritual development. Recognizing its presence and impact is essential for breaking free from its constraints and embarking on a journey toward self-discovery, authenticity, and genuine fulfillment. By seeking God's approval above all else, embracing our uniqueness, and fostering a healthy sense of self-worth, we can gradually overcome the fear of judgment and experience a life marked by courage, purpose, and unwavering faith.

Recognizing the Fear of Judgment and Its Impact: Biblical truth in Illuminating Pathways to Liberation

The fear of judgment is a deeply rooted and pervasive emotion that often stealthily influences our thoughts, actions, and decisions. Stemming from the innate human desire for acceptance and validation, this fear manifests when we anticipate criticism, rejection, or disapproval from others. While a certain level of concern about others' opinions is normal, an overwhelming fear of judgment can have a profound impact on our well-being, hinder personal growth, and distort our authentic identity. Recognizing the fear of judgment and understanding its far-reaching consequences is a crucial step toward breaking its hold and forging a path to liberation and genuine self-expression.

1. Self-Censorship and Authenticity

The fear of judgment often leads to self-censorship, causing us to withhold our true thoughts, feelings, and aspirations. Galatians 1:10 (NIV) poignantly addresses this issue: "Am I now trying to win the approval of human beings, or of God? Or am I trying to please people? If I were still trying to please people, I would not be a servant of Christ." When we prioritize human validation over authentic self-expression, we risk diluting our true essence and stifling the unique voice God has gifted us.

2. Diminished Self-Esteem

Constant concern about others' opinions can erode our self-esteem and self-worth. Psalm 139:14 (NIV) offers a counter-narrative: "I praise you because I am fearfully and wonderfully made; your works are wonderful; I know that full well." Succumbing to the fear of judgment fosters negative self-talk, fuels self-doubt, and impairs our ability to fully embrace our God-given potential.

3. Impact on Relationships

The fear of judgment can strain relationships as we modify our behavior and opinions to avoid criticism or rejection. Romans 12:2 (NIV) advises against conforming to the world's patterns: "Do not conform to the pattern of this world, but be transformed by the renewing of your mind." Authentic connections are compromised when we prioritize external approval over genuine connection, leading to strained interactions and missed opportunities for deeper relationships.

4. Missed Opportunities and Growth

A pervasive fear of judgment can lead to missed opportunities for personal and spiritual growth. Jeremiah 29:11 (NIV) assures us of God's plans: "For I know the plans I have for you, declares the Lord, plans to prosper you and not to harm you, plans to give you hope and a future." Allowing fear to dictate decisions prevents us from stepping into new challenges, acquiring new skills, and fulfilling God's purpose for our lives.

5. Hindrance to Spiritual Progress

The fear of judgment can hinder our spiritual progress by diverting our focus from God's approval to human validation. Proverbs 29:25 (NIV) reminds us of the consequences of fear: "Fear of man will prove to be a snare, but whoever trusts in the Lord is kept safe." This fear can lead us away from God's intended path, weakening our relationship with Him and compromising our spiritual journey.

6. Emotional Toll

The fear of judgment exacts an emotional toll, often resulting in stress, anxiety, and emotional turmoil. Matthew 6:34 (NIV) encourages us not to be anxious: "Therefore do not worry about tomorrow, for tomorrow will worry about itself. Each day has enough trouble of its own." This constant anxiety and worry can negatively impact our mental and physical well-being.

7. Misaligned Identity

Constantly seeking external validation can lead to a misaligned sense of identity. Ephesians 2:10 (NIV) affirms our identity as God's handiwork: "For we are God's handiwork, created in Christ Jesus to do good works, which God prepared in advance for us to do." When we prioritize others' opinions over God's purpose, we risk losing sight of our true identity and unique role in God's plan.

Conclusion

Recognizing the fear of judgment and its far-reaching impact is the first step toward liberation and authenticity. By embracing our identity in Christ, grounding ourselves in God's unwavering love, and aligning our actions with His purpose, we can overcome the fear of judgment. Through God's guidance and a renewed perspective, we can break free from the chains of external validation, walk confidently in our true identity, and contribute authentically to the world around us.

5.2 Challenging negative self-talk

Challenging Negative Self-Talk: Transforming Your Inner Dialogue for Positive Change

The power of words is undeniable. They have the ability to shape our perceptions, influence our emotions, and impact our actions. Yet, one of the most influential conversations we engage in is often the one we have with ourselves. This internal dialogue, known as self-talk, has a profound impact on our self-esteem, confidence, and overall well-being. Unfortunately, for many individuals, this self-talk can often turn negative, leading to self-doubt, insecurity, and a hindered sense of progress. However, by understanding the nature of negative self-talk, its origins, and implementing strategies to challenge and transform it, we can unlock a pathway to positive change, improved mental health, and greater self-empowerment.

Understanding Negative Self-Talk

Negative self-talk involves the habit of using pessimistic, critical, or defeatist language when speaking to oneself. It often takes the form of self-criticism, self-blame, and self-doubt. This internal dialogue is influenced by various factors, including past experiences, societal pressures, and personal beliefs. Negative self-talk can become an automatic response, occurring without conscious awareness and perpetuating a cycle of negativity.

Origins of Negative Self-Talk

Negative self-talk can originate from a variety of sources:

1. Early Experiences: Childhood experiences, criticism, or comparison to others can contribute to the development of negative self-perceptions that persist into adulthood.

2. Social Comparisons: Constantly comparing oneself to others, especially in the age of social media, can foster feelings of inadequacy and self-criticism.

3. Perfectionism: Striving for perfection and setting unrealistic standards can lead to a constant sense of falling short, fueling negative self-talk.

4. Fear of Failure: A fear of failure can generate self-doubt and harsh self-judgment, magnifying negative self-talk during challenging situations.

5. Negative Feedback Loop: When negative thoughts go unchallenged, they reinforce themselves, creating a self-perpetuating cycle of negativity.

The Impact of Negative Self-Talk

The impact of negative self-talk is far-reaching:

1. Self-Esteem: Negative self-talk chips away at self-esteem, making it difficult to believe in oneself and one's abilities.

2. Confidence: A constant stream of self-criticism undermines confidence, hindering the pursuit of goals and new experiences.
3. Mental Health: Negative self-talk is closely linked to anxiety, depression, and other mental health challenges.
4. Decision-Making: Negative self-talk can cloud judgment, leading to poor decision-making and avoidance of opportunities.
5. Relationships: Self-doubt can affect how we interact with others, potentially straining relationships.

Strategies to Challenge Negative Self-Talk

Transforming negative self-talk requires conscious effort and a commitment to self-compassion and growth. Here are effective strategies:

1. Mindfulness and Awareness: Begin by becoming mindful of your self-talk. Observe your thoughts without judgment, identifying patterns of negativity.
2. Reframing: Replace negative thoughts with realistic and balanced ones. Challenge the accuracy of negative assumptions.
3. Self-Compassion: Treat yourself with the same kindness and understanding you'd offer a friend. Use encouraging, self-compassionate language.
4. Evidence-Based Thinking: Assess the evidence for and against negative self-talk. Often, negative assumptions lack a solid foundation.
5. Positive Affirmations: Intentionally replace negative thoughts with positive affirmations that reflect your true worth and potential.
6. Gratitude Practice: Cultivate a habit of focusing on what you are grateful for, shifting your mindset away from negativity.
7. Limit Comparisons: Avoid comparing yourself to others. Focus on your own progress and growth.
8. Seek Support: Share your struggles with trusted friends, family, or professionals who can provide encouragement and perspective.

Biblical Insights on Challenging Negative Self-Talk

The Bible offers wisdom that aligns with the journey of challenging negative self-talk:

1. Philippians 4:8 (NIV): "Finally, brothers and sisters, whatever is true, whatever is noble, whatever is right, whatever is pure, whatever is lovely, whatever is admirable—if anything is

excellent or praiseworthy—think about such things." This verse emphasizes the importance of focusing on positive, uplifting thoughts.

2. Psalm 139:14 (NIV): "I praise you because I am fearfully and wonderfully made; your works are wonderful; I know that full well." Acknowledge your inherent worth as a creation of God.

3. 2 Corinthians 10:5 (NIV): "We demolish arguments and every pretension that sets itself up against the knowledge of God, and we take captive every thought to make it obedient to Christ." This verse encourages the practice of taking control of our thoughts and aligning them with God's truth.

Therefore, challenging negative self-talk is a transformative journey that empowers us to break free from the limitations of self-doubt and embrace a more positive and empowering internal dialogue. By recognizing the origins of negative self-talk, understanding its impact, and implementing strategic approaches rooted in mindfulness, self-compassion, and evidence-based thinking, we can reshape our thought patterns and unlock a pathway to greater self-empowerment, improved mental health, and a deeper connection with our true potential. In aligning our thoughts with God's truth and love, we can embark on a journey of lasting positive change and renewed self-confidence.

Challenging Negative Self-Talk: Empowering Your Mind with Biblical Wisdom

Negative self-talk is a formidable barrier that can hinder personal growth, erode self-esteem, and impede one's pursuit of purpose. It is an internal dialogue that often consists of self-criticism, self-doubt, and pessimism, leading to a cycle of negativity. However, through the lens of Biblical wisdom, we can uncover powerful strategies to challenge and transform this destructive pattern, replacing it with a mindset rooted in God's truth and love.

1. Acknowledging God's Creation

Psalm 139:14 (NIV) reminds us, "I praise you because I am fearfully and wonderfully made; your works are wonderful, I know that full well." Embracing our identity as creations of a loving and intentional God helps counter negative self-talk. Recognizing our inherent worth and uniqueness as products of divine craftsmanship enables us to challenge thoughts that undermine our self-esteem.

2. Renewing the Mind

Romans 12:2 (NIV) encourages us, "Do not conform to the pattern of this world, but be transformed by the renewing of your mind. Then you will be able to test and approve what God's will is—his good, pleasing and perfect will." By intentionally renewing our minds with God's truth, we can counter negative self-talk with thoughts aligned with His purpose and plan for our lives.

3. Guarding Your Heart

Proverbs 4:23 (NIV) advises, "Above all else, guard your heart, for everything you do flows from it." Negative self-talk often originates from a heart burdened by insecurities and past wounds. By safeguarding our hearts through prayer, meditation, and immersion in Scripture, we create a protective barrier against harmful self-talk and foster an environment of God's peace and love.

4. Taking Captive Every Thought

2 Corinthians 10:5 (NIV) teaches us, "We demolish arguments and every pretension that sets itself up against the knowledge of God, and we take captive every thought to make it obedient to Christ." This verse empowers us to actively challenge negative thoughts, subjecting them to the authority of Christ's truth. By examining our thoughts in light of God's Word, we can identify and replace untruths with His promises.

5. Focusing on the Positive

Philippians 4:8 (NIV) instructs, "Finally, brothers and sisters, whatever is true, whatever is noble, whatever is right, whatever is pure, whatever is lovely, whatever is admirable—if anything is excellent or praiseworthy—think about such things." Cultivating a mindset centered on positivity, gratitude, and God's attributes counters the grip of negative self-talk and fosters a healthier thought life.

6. Embracing God's Unchanging Love

Romans 8:38-39 (NIV) affirms, "For I am convinced that neither death nor life, neither angels nor demons, neither the present nor the future, nor any powers, neither height nor depth, nor anything else in all creation, will be able to separate us from the love of God that is in Christ Jesus our Lord." Anchoring ourselves in God's unwavering love enables us to challenge negative self-talk by embracing the truth of our unbreakable connection with Him.

7. Affirming Your Identity in Christ

Galatians 2:20 (NIV) declares, "I have been crucified with Christ and I no longer live, but Christ lives in me. The life I now live in the body, I live by faith in the Son of God, who loved me and gave himself for me." As believers, our identity is rooted in Christ. When negative self-talk tries to undermine our worth, we can affirm our identity as cherished children of God.

Conclusion

Challenging negative self-talk is a transformative journey that requires consistent effort and alignment with God's truth. By drawing strength from Scripture and embracing God's perspective on our worth, purpose, and identity, we can counter the harmful effects of negative self-talk. As we intentionally renew our minds, guard our hearts, and take captive every thought, we create a fertile ground for God's love, grace, and purpose to flourish. Through this journey, we not only conquer negative self-talk but also cultivate a mindset that empowers us to live authentically, pursue our God-given potential, and walk confidently in the light of His truth.

5.3 Surrounding yourself with a supportive network

Surrounding Yourself with a Supportive Network: Nurturing Growth, Resilience, and Well-Being

The journey of life is not meant to be traversed alone. Just as a tree needs a rich soil to thrive, humans need a nurturing environment to flourish. Surrounding yourself with a supportive network is a pivotal component of personal growth, resilience, and overall well-being. A supportive network consists of individuals who uplift, encourage, and stand by you through life's challenges and triumphs. This network provides emotional sustenance, practical guidance, and a sense of belonging, creating a foundation upon which you can cultivate your potential and navigate the complexities of life.

1. Emotional Reservoir

A supportive network serves as an emotional reservoir, offering a safe space to express feelings, fears, and aspirations without judgment. In times of hardship, having someone to confide in provides solace and alleviates emotional burdens. Proverbs 17:17 (NIV) captures the essence of such relationships: "A friend loves at all times, and a brother is born for a time of adversity." A friend's presence during adversity reinforces the sense of solidarity and offers a shoulder to lean on.

2. Encouragement and Motivation

Surrounding yourself with a supportive network fuels motivation and encourages growth. 1 Thessalonians 5:11 (NIV) underscores the importance of encouragement: "Therefore encourage one another and build each other up, just as in fact you are doing." A network that believes in your potential and offers words of encouragement spurs you on to pursue your dreams and overcome challenges with renewed determination.

3. Diverse Perspectives

A diverse network brings together individuals with varying perspectives, experiences, and expertise. Proverbs 15:22 (NIV) highlights the wisdom of seeking counsel: "Plans fail for lack of counsel, but with many advisers they succeed." Engaging with a variety of viewpoints broadens your horizons, facilitates informed decision-making, and fosters personal growth through exposure to new ideas.

4. Skill Development

A supportive network can aid in skill development by sharing knowledge, insights, and experiences. Whether learning a new skill or seeking guidance in a particular area, mentors and peers within your network can offer guidance and practical tips. Ecclesiastes 4:9-10 (NIV) emphasizes the value of mutual support: "Two are better than one, because they have a good return for their labor: If either of them falls down, one can help the other up."

5. Resilience and Coping

Life's challenges are inevitable, but a strong network enhances your ability to cope and bounce back. Romans 12:15 (NIV) highlights the significance of shared experiences: "Rejoice with those who rejoice; mourn with those who mourn." A supportive network stands by you in times of sorrow, reinforcing your emotional resilience and demonstrating that you are not alone in facing difficulties.

6. Celebration of Achievements

A network that genuinely celebrates your achievements cultivates a sense of validation and belonging. Galatians 6:2 (NIV) speaks to bearing each other's burdens: "Carry each other's burdens, and in this way, you will fulfill the law of Christ." Just as burdens are shared, so too are joys. Sharing successes with a supportive network reinforces a sense of accomplishment and reminds you that your efforts are recognized and valued.

7. Fostering Mutual Growth

A supportive network operates on a reciprocal basis, where each member contributes to the growth and well-being of others. Proverbs 27:17 (NIV) illustrates this concept: "As iron sharpens iron, so one person sharpens another." The synergy of like-minded individuals striving for growth propels each member forward, creating an environment where mutual encouragement and accountability thrive.

Note: Surrounding yourself with a supportive network is a deliberate and transformative choice that enriches your journey through life. Through emotional nourishment, encouragement, diverse perspectives, skill development, resilience, shared celebrations, and mutual growth, a network acts as a catalyst for personal development and overall well-being. As you cultivate these relationships, you create a tapestry of connections that uplift, inspire, and empower you to embrace your potential, face challenges with courage, and experience the joy of walking through life's ups and downs with companions who genuinely care and stand by your side.

Surrounding Yourself with a Supportive Network: Biblical Insights into Nurturing Relationships

God's design for human connection and community is evident throughout the Bible. The importance of surrounding yourself with a supportive network is deeply rooted in Scripture, offering wisdom and guidance on how meaningful relationships contribute to personal growth, resilience, and spiritual well-being.

1. God's Plan for Fellowship

Genesis 2:18 (NIV) reveals the origin of human companionship: "The Lord God said, 'It is not good for the man to be alone. I will make a helper suitable for him.'" From the very beginning, God recognized the need for human connection and companionship. Surrounding yourself with a supportive network aligns with God's intention for us to share life's journey with others.

2. Iron Sharpens Iron

Proverbs 27:17 (NIV) emphasizes the positive influence of relationships: "As iron sharpens iron, so one person sharpens another." Just as two pieces of iron refine each other's edges, meaningful relationships enable growth, learning, and mutual support. A supportive network encourages personal and spiritual development, inspiring individuals to strive for excellence.

3. Mutual Encouragement

Hebrews 10:24-25 (NIV) underscores the value of communal encouragement: "And let us consider how we may spur one another on toward love and good deeds, not giving up meeting together, as some are in the habit of doing, but encouraging one another—and all the more as you see the Day approaching." Within a supportive network, individuals uplift each other, fostering a culture of positivity and shared aspirations.

4. Bearing Burdens Together

Galatians 6:2 (NIV) highlights the importance of sharing life's challenges: "Carry each other's burdens, and in this way, you will fulfill the law of Christ." A network that stands by you during difficult times provides emotional strength and resilience. Knowing that you are not alone in your struggles lessens the weight of burdens and reinforces your ability to overcome adversity.

5. Accountability and Growth

Ecclesiastes 4:9-10 (NIV) speaks to the power of unity: "Two are better than one, because they have a good return for their labor: If either of them falls down, one can help the other up." A supportive network fosters accountability, pushing individuals to pursue growth, overcome obstacles, and achieve goals. This shared journey of progress creates an environment conducive to personal and spiritual development.

6. Loving One Another

John 13:34-35 (NIV) emphasizes the importance of love within a community: "A new command I give you: Love one another. As I have loved you, so you must love one another. By this everyone will know that you are my disciples, if you love one another." A supportive network is grounded in love, reflecting the very essence of Christ's teachings and embodying His example of compassion and care.

7. Mutual Prayer and Intercession

James 5:16 (NIV) encourages the practice of mutual prayer: "Therefore confess your sins to each other and pray for each other so that you may be healed. The prayer of a righteous person is powerful and effective." A supportive network provides a space for intercession, where members can lift each other's concerns to God, fostering spiritual growth and unity.

Conclusion

Surrounding yourself with a supportive network is a fundamental principle deeply embedded in the fabric of the Christian faith. Through mutual encouragement, accountability, shared burdens, love, and prayer, a supportive network creates an environment conducive to personal and spiritual growth. As you cultivate these relationships, you are not only fostering your own well-being but also living out God's design for interconnectedness and community. Just as the early disciples supported and strengthened one another, you too can experience the transformative power of meaningful relationships, walking hand in hand with fellow believers on a journey of faith, growth, and shared purpose.

5.4 The power of vulnerability and authenticity

The Power of Vulnerability and Authenticity: Embracing True Connection and Growth

In a world often dominated by façades and pretenses, the power of vulnerability and authenticity shines as a beacon of genuine human connection, personal growth, and emotional well-being. Vulnerability is the courage to show up as our true selves, flaws and all, while authenticity is the consistent alignment of our actions with our values and beliefs. Together, they create a transformative force that enriches relationships, fosters personal development, and cultivates a profound sense of fulfillment.

1. Authenticity Breeds Connection

When we allow ourselves to be vulnerable and authentic, we create an environment where others feel safe to do the same. Authenticity nurtures genuine connections by signaling trustworthiness and sincerity. When people perceive that someone is being their true self, it often encourages them to let down their own guard, facilitating deeper and more meaningful relationships.

2. Breaking Down Barriers

Vulnerability has the remarkable power to dissolve emotional barriers that hinder authentic connections. By sharing our struggles, fears, and insecurities, we demonstrate our humanity and invite others to do the same. This raw openness creates a space where people can relate on a deeper level, leading to empathy, understanding, and a stronger sense of camaraderie.

3. Encouraging Growth

Authenticity propels personal growth by challenging us to confront our true desires, strengths, and weaknesses. When we live authentically, we engage in self-reflection, embracing our true identity and setting the stage for transformative change. As we recognize our areas for growth and work towards them, we create a fulfilling and purpose-driven life.

4. Fostering Emotional Resilience

Vulnerability and authenticity also contribute to emotional resilience. By acknowledging and expressing our feelings, we develop a greater capacity to handle challenges and bounce back from adversity. The act of sharing our vulnerabilities can alleviate emotional burdens, promoting mental and emotional well-being.

5. Empowering Others

Our vulnerability and authenticity have the power to inspire others to embrace their own true selves. When people witness someone embracing their imperfections and living authentically, it sends a powerful message that it's okay to be oneself. This empowerment creates a ripple effect, encouraging others to shed societal expectations and embrace their uniqueness.

6. Authentic Leadership

Authenticity is a hallmark of effective leadership. Leaders who are willing to admit their mistakes, share their struggles, and express genuine emotions foster a culture of openness and trust within their teams. This, in turn, leads to increased employee engagement, loyalty, and collaboration.

7. Emotional Connection and Fulfillment

Authenticity and vulnerability strengthen emotional connections in relationships, be it friendships, romantic partnerships, or family bonds. When people share their true thoughts, feelings, and experiences, it fosters intimacy and a sense of closeness. This emotional connection enhances the overall quality of relationships and contributes to a greater sense of fulfillment.

Conclusion

The power of vulnerability and authenticity lies in their ability to transcend societal expectations, fear of judgment, and self-doubt. By embracing our true selves, sharing our stories, and connecting on a deeper level, we create an environment of trust, empathy, and mutual support. This fosters personal growth, emotional well-being, and enriches the tapestry of our lives with genuine, meaningful connections. As we allow ourselves to be vulnerable and authentic, we embark on a transformative journey that leads to a more fulfilling, purpose-driven, and interconnected existence.

The Power of Vulnerability and Authenticity: A Biblical Perspective on True Connection and Growth

Vulnerability and authenticity are potent forces that resonate deeply with the teachings of the Bible, offering profound insights into the nature of human connection, personal growth, and spiritual transformation. Rooted in the Gospel message of love, grace, and embracing one's true self, the power of vulnerability and authenticity is illuminated through various passages that encourage believers to forge genuine relationships, foster growth, and draw closer to God.

**1. Strength in Weakness

2 Corinthians 12:9-10 (NIV) exemplifies the paradox of vulnerability: "But he said to me, 'My grace is sufficient for you, for my power is made perfect in weakness.' Therefore, I will boast all the more gladly about my weaknesses, so that Christ's power may rest on me. That is why, for Christ's sake, I delight in weaknesses, in insults, in hardships, in persecutions, in difficulties. For when I am weak, then I am strong." This passage emphasizes that acknowledging our weaknesses and vulnerabilities not only invites Christ's strength but also transforms them into sources of empowerment.

2. Mutual Encouragement

Hebrews 10:24-25 (NIV) underscores the importance of authentic community: "And let us consider how we may spur one another on toward love and good deeds, not giving up meeting together, as some are in the habit of doing, but encouraging one another—and all the more as you see the Day approaching." Here, vulnerability and authenticity are integral to mutual encouragement, motivating believers to uplift and support each other on their faith journeys.

3. Bearing One Another's Burdens

Galatians 6:2 (NIV) emphasizes the shared responsibility of vulnerability: "Carry each other's burdens, and in this way, you will fulfill the law of Christ." When we open ourselves to others and allow them to share our burdens, we embody Christ's love and exemplify the power of authentic connection in overcoming life's challenges.

4. A Broken and Contrite Heart

Psalm 51:17 (NIV) highlights the significance of authenticity in our relationship with God: "My sacrifice, O God, is a broken spirit; a broken and contrite heart you, God, will not despise." True authenticity involves humbling ourselves before God, acknowledging our imperfections, and seeking His mercy and transformation.

5. True Identity in Christ

Ephesians 2:10 (NIV) affirms our unique identity in Christ: "For we are God's handiwork, created in Christ Jesus to do good works, which God prepared in advance for us to do." Embracing vulnerability and authenticity enables us to live out this identity, free from the need to conform to worldly expectations and focused on fulfilling God's purpose for our lives.

6. Confession and Healing

James 5:16 (NIV) emphasizes the healing power of vulnerability: "Therefore confess your sins to each other and pray for each other so that you may be healed. The prayer of a righteous person is powerful and effective." Authentic confession, rooted in vulnerability, paves the way for spiritual and emotional healing, both individually and within the body of believers.

7. Love and Unity

1 Corinthians 12:25-26 (NIV) underscores the interconnectedness of believers: "so that there should be no division in the body, but that its parts should have equal concern for each other. If one part suffers, every part suffers with it; if one part is honored, every part rejoices with it." Vulnerability and authenticity foster an environment of love and unity, where the joys and sorrows of each individual are shared by the entire community.

Conclusion

The power of vulnerability and authenticity, as exemplified through these biblical passages, serves as a guiding light for believers seeking deeper connections, personal growth, and spiritual transformation. By embracing our weaknesses, sharing burdens, seeking God's healing, and fostering authentic relationships, we tap into a wellspring of grace and strength that empowers us to live in alignment with our true selves and our faith. Just as Jesus embraced vulnerability on the cross for the sake of humanity, we too are called to lay aside our masks, open our hearts, and experience the transformative power of vulnerability and authenticity in our relationships with God and one another.

CHAPTER SIX
TAKING ACTION AND EMBRACING FAILURE

Taking Action and Embracing Failure

Taking Action and Embracing Failure: The Path to Growth and Success

In the journey of life, taking action and embracing failure are two pivotal elements that propel us forward, leading to personal growth, resilience, and ultimately, success. These two concepts are deeply intertwined, as the willingness to take action often entails the acceptance of potential failure. By understanding their dynamic relationship and cultivating a mindset that embraces both, we open doors to new opportunities, learning experiences, and a fulfilling life journey.

Taking Action

Taking action is the catalyst that transforms dreams and aspirations into reality. It involves stepping out of one's comfort zone, making decisions, and initiating steps towards a desired goal. Procrastination and indecision can hinder progress, whereas action empowers us to make tangible strides towards achieving our objectives.

1. Overcoming Inertia

The principle of taking action is reflected in Proverbs 14:23 (NIV): "All hard work brings a profit, but mere talk leads only to poverty." This verse underscores the value of diligent effort and emphasizes that progress comes from taking tangible steps, not just from empty words or intentions.

2. Cultivating Initiative

In the parable of the talents (Matthew 25:14-30), Jesus teaches the importance of using and multiplying our gifts. The two servants who took action and invested their talents were rewarded, while the one who buried his talent out of fear faced consequences. This parable highlights the significance of initiative and the potential for growth that comes from taking action.

Embracing Failure

Embracing failure is an essential mindset shift that reframes setbacks as opportunities for growth and learning. Failure is not a final destination but a stepping stone on the path to success. Through failure, we gain valuable insights, develop resilience, and refine our approach.

1. Learning from Mistakes

Proverbs 24:16 (NIV) acknowledges the inevitability of failure: "for though the righteous fall seven times, they rise again." This verse illustrates that even the most virtuous individuals face challenges and setbacks. Embracing failure involves learning from mistakes, getting back up, and continuing the journey with renewed determination.

2. Resilience and Perseverance

James 1:2-4 (NIV) encourages perseverance through trials: "Consider it pure joy, my brothers and sisters, whenever you face trials of many kinds, because you know that the testing of your faith produces perseverance. Let perseverance finish its work so that you may be mature and complete, not lacking anything." Embracing failure fosters resilience, allowing us to withstand challenges and emerge stronger.

3. Innovating and Adapting

Failure often prompts us to reassess our approach and explore innovative solutions. The apostle Paul's journey in spreading the Gospel exemplifies this adaptability. When faced with obstacles, he adjusted his strategies while remaining steadfast in his mission. Failure can lead to creative thinking and the discovery of new paths to success.

Hence, taking action and embracing failure are essential components of a purposeful and successful life journey. They are intertwined threads that form the fabric of growth, resilience, and achievement. By taking action, we propel ourselves forward, transform possibilities into realities, and actively engage with life's opportunities. Embracing failure allows us to learn, adapt, and ultimately thrive in the face of challenges. Both concepts align with biblical teachings, reminding us that diligence, initiative, and perseverance are central to living a life that honors our potential and purpose. As we step out in faith, take action, and embrace failure as a teacher, we embark on a transformative voyage of self-discovery, growth, and the fulfillment of God's plan for our lives.

Taking Action and Embracing Failure: Biblical Wisdom for Growth and Resilience

In the journey of life, taking action and embracing failure are two essential pillars that propel us toward personal growth, success, and spiritual maturity. Rooted in biblical principles, these concepts offer profound insights into how we can navigate challenges, overcome obstacles, and fulfill our God-given potential.

Taking Action

1. Faith in Action

James 2:17 (NIV) emphasizes the significance of taking action as an expression of faith: "In the same way, faith by itself, if it is not accompanied by action, is dead." This verse underscores that faith is not merely a passive belief, but a catalyst for action. Our actions demonstrate the authenticity of our faith and our willingness to trust God's guidance.

2. Stepping Out in Obedience

Abraham's obedience and action in response to God's call serve as a powerful example. Hebrews 11:8 (NIV) states, "By faith Abraham, when called to go to a place he would later receive as his inheritance, obeyed and went, even though he did not know where he was going." Abraham's willingness to take action, despite uncertainty, showcased his faith and paved the way for God's promises to be fulfilled.

3. The Parable of the Talents

Matthew 25:14-30 presents the Parable of the Talents, illustrating the importance of investing our gifts and talents through action. The servants who took action and multiplied their talents were commended, while the one who buried his talent faced consequences.

This parable underscores the principle that taking action is a stewardship of the resources and opportunities entrusted to us.
Embracing Failure
1. Learning Through Humility

Proverbs 16:18 (NIV) cautions against pride and highlights the lessons of failure: "Pride goes before destruction, a haughty spirit before a fall." Embracing failure requires humility—acknowledging that we are not infallible and that our growth often stems from learning through mistakes and setbacks.
2. God's Grace in Weakness

2 Corinthians 12:9 (NIV) offers comfort and perspective in times of failure: "But he said to me, 'My grace is sufficient for you, for my power is made perfect in weakness.' Therefore, I will boast all the more gladly about my weaknesses, so that Christ's power may rest on me." Embracing failure allows us to rely on God's grace and recognize His strength in our moments of weakness.
3. Perseverance and Character

Romans 5:3-4 (NIV) speaks to the growth that arises from adversity: "Not only so, but we also glory in our sufferings, because we know that suffering produces perseverance; perseverance, character; and character, hope." Embracing failure as part of our journey contributes to the development of perseverance, character, and a hopeful outlook.
4. Redemption Through Christ

Romans 8:28 (NIV) assures believers of God's redemptive power even in failure: "And we know that in all things God works for the good of those who love him, who have been called according to his purpose." Embracing failure with faith allows us to trust that God can use even our setbacks for His ultimate purpose and plan.
Conclusion

Taking action and embracing failure, when grounded in biblical wisdom, lead to a holistic approach to personal growth and resilience. Through action, we live out our faith, honor our stewardship, and actively participate in God's purposes. Embracing failure with humility and trust in God's grace allows us to learn, grow, and ultimately emerge stronger. These concepts intertwine to form a transformative journey— one marked by faith-filled steps, courageous endeavors, and a steadfast reliance on God's guidance through both successes and failures. As we navigate life's challenges with a heart willing to take action and embrace failure's lessons, we draw closer to the fullness of God's intended blessings for our lives.

6.1 Overcoming procrastination and analysis paralysis

Overcoming Procrastination and Analysis Paralysis: Unleashing Productivity and Progress

Procrastination and analysis paralysis are two formidable obstacles that hinder personal growth, hinder productivity, and impede the pursuit of goals. Both are characterized by an inability to take decisive action, whether due to fear of failure, perfectionism, or excessive contemplation. Overcoming these challenges requires a combination of mindset shifts, practical strategies, and intentional efforts to reclaim control over one's time, energy, and aspirations.

Understanding Procrastination

Procrastination is the act of postponing tasks or actions that need to be accomplished. It often stems from a variety of underlying factors, such as fear of failure, lack of motivation, or a sense of being overwhelmed by the enormity of a task. Procrastination can lead to wasted opportunities, increased stress, and a cycle of self-doubt.

1. Reframing Mindset

A key step in overcoming procrastination is cultivating a proactive mindset. Philippians 4:13 (NIV) encourages believers: "I can do all this through him who gives me strength." By shifting our perspective to one of empowerment and reliance on God's strength, we can overcome the mental barriers that contribute to procrastination.

2. Taking Small Steps

Procrastination often results from feeling daunted by the magnitude of a task. Breaking tasks into smaller, manageable steps can make them feel less overwhelming. Proverbs 13:4 (NIV) reflects this principle: "A sluggard's appetite is never filled, but the desires of the diligent are fully satisfied." Taking consistent, small actions gradually leads to a sense of achievement and progress.

Understanding Analysis Paralysis

Analysis paralysis, on the other hand, occurs when individuals become trapped in a cycle of overthinking and excessive analysis. It can lead to indecision, delayed action, and missed opportunities. Striving for perfection or fearing making the wrong choice are common triggers of analysis paralysis.

1. Trusting Divine Guidance

Proverbs 3:5-6 (NIV) provides guidance on decision-making: "Trust in the Lord with all your heart and lean not on your own understanding; in all your ways submit to him, and he will make your paths straight." Relying on God's wisdom and seeking His guidance can help overcome the inclination to endlessly analyze and instead move forward with confidence.

2. Setting Time Limits

A practical strategy to combat analysis paralysis is setting time limits for decision-making. Ecclesiastes 3:1 (NIV) emphasizes the importance of timing: "There is a time for everything, and a season for every activity under the heavens." Establishing deadlines for making choices prevents prolonged deliberation and encourages timely action.

3. Embracing Imperfection

Perfectionism often fuels analysis paralysis. Recognizing that perfection is unattainable and that mistakes are part of the journey is essential. 2 Corinthians 12:9 (NIV) reminds us of God's grace in weakness: "My grace is sufficient for you, for my power is made perfect in weakness." Embracing imperfection allows us to move forward without the weight of unrealistic expectations.

Accordingly, overcoming procrastination and analysis paralysis requires a holistic approach that encompasses mindset shifts, practical strategies, and reliance on spiritual guidance. By reframing our mindset, breaking tasks into smaller steps, trusting in God's wisdom, setting time limits, and embracing imperfection, we can free ourselves from the shackles of inaction. Proverbs 16:3 (NIV) encapsulates the essence of overcoming these challenges: "Commit to the Lord whatever you do, and he will establish your plans." Through intentional effort and faith, we can break free from the grip of procrastination and analysis paralysis, unleashing our potential, productivity, and progress in pursuit of our goals and God's purpose for our lives.

Overcoming Procrastination and Analysis Paralysis: A Biblical Perspective on Productivity and Decision-Making

Procrastination and analysis paralysis are common challenges that can hinder personal growth, hinder progress, and impede the fulfillment of God's purposes for our lives. However, through biblical principles, wisdom, and actionable strategies, we can overcome these obstacles and step into a life of purpose, productivity, and confident decision-making.

Overcoming Procrastination

1. Stewardship of Time

Ephesians 5:15-16 (NIV) exhorts us to wisely manage our time: "Be very careful, then, how you live—not as unwise but as wise, making the most of every opportunity, because the days are evil." Recognizing time as a precious resource entrusted to us by God can motivate us to overcome procrastination and prioritize tasks that align with His will.

2. Diligence and Persistence

Proverbs 21:5 (NIV) emphasizes the value of diligence: "The plans of the diligent lead to profit as surely as haste leads to poverty." Diligence involves consistent effort and focused action, which can counteract the tendency to procrastinate. By persistently working towards our goals, we honor God's call to be faithful stewards of the talents He has given us.

3. Relying on God's Strength

Philippians 4:13 (NIV) assures us that we can accomplish tasks through Christ's strength: "I can do all this through him who gives me strength." This verse reminds us that our abilities are not limited to our own, and we can overcome procrastination by relying on God's empowering grace to take action.

Overcoming Analysis Paralysis

1. Seeking God's Wisdom

James 1:5 (NIV) encourages seeking divine wisdom in decision-making: "If any of you lacks wisdom, you should ask God, who gives generously to all without finding fault, and it will be given to you." When faced with analysis paralysis, turning to God in prayer and seeking His guidance can provide clarity and direction.

2. Trusting God's Providence

Proverbs 16:9 (NIV) reminds us of God's sovereign control over our plans: "In their hearts humans plan their course, but the Lord establishes their steps." While thoughtful consideration is important, ultimately, we can trust that God directs our paths and can guide us through analysis paralysis to make sound decisions.

3. Embracing Faith over Fear

2 Timothy 1:7 (NIV) encourages us to embrace faith over fear: "For the Spirit God gave us does not make us timid, but gives us power, love and self-discipline." Analysis paralysis often stems from fear of making the wrong choice. By relying on the Spirit's power and exercising self-discipline, we can overcome fear and move forward confidently.

4. Taking Action with Purpose

James 2:17 (NIV) highlights the importance of combining faith and action: "In the same way, faith by itself, if it is not accompanied by action, is dead." Taking purposeful steps, even if they involve calculated risks, reflects an active faith that can break the cycle of overthinking and analysis paralysis.

Conclusion

Overcoming procrastination and analysis paralysis requires aligning our actions and decisions with biblical principles. By stewarding our time, diligently pursuing tasks, relying on God's strength, seeking His wisdom, trusting in His providence, embracing faith over fear, and taking purposeful action, we can break free from these hindrances. Through these practices, we can walk in obedience to God's calling, cultivate a life of purposeful productivity, and make decisions that honor Him and advance His kingdom. As we surrender our tendencies to procrastinate and overanalyze, we open ourselves to experiencing God's abundant blessings and fulfilling our unique roles in His divine plan.

6.2 Learning from failure and turning setbacks into opportunities

Learning from Failure and Turning Setbacks into Opportunities: A Path of Growth and Resilience

Failure and setbacks are inevitable aspects of life, often met with disappointment and frustration. However, these challenges need not be the end of the road; rather, they can serve as valuable stepping stones toward personal growth, resilience, and the discovery of new opportunities. By adopting a proactive mindset and embracing the lessons that failure offers, individuals can transform setbacks into catalysts for positive change and advancement.

Embracing the Lessons of Failure

1. Reflection and Self-Awareness

Failure provides an opportunity for deep self-reflection and self-awareness. By analyzing what went wrong and why, individuals gain insights into their strengths, weaknesses, and areas for improvement. This process of introspection contributes to personal growth and enhances one's ability to navigate future challenges.

2. Humility and Resilience

Proverbs 16:18 (NIV) reminds us, "Pride goes before destruction, a haughty spirit before a fall." Failure humbles us, reminding us of our human limitations and encouraging us to approach life with humility. This humility, coupled with the determination to rise again, fosters resilience—a vital trait that enables us to bounce back from setbacks.

3. Paving the Way for Success

Failure often guides us toward the path of success by highlighting what doesn't work. Thomas Edison famously stated, "I have not failed. I've just found 10,000 ways that won't work." Each failed attempt brings us closer to uncovering effective strategies, making the eventual achievement all the more rewarding.

Turning Setbacks into Opportunities

1. Reframing and Adaptation

Romans 8:28 (NIV) offers assurance: "And we know that in all things God works for the good of those who love him, who have been called according to his purpose." Even setbacks can be used for good. By reframing failures as opportunities for growth and adaptation, individuals can pivot their approach and discover new ways to succeed.

2. Fostering Creativity

Setbacks force us to think outside the box and explore alternative solutions. Just as Joseph's trials led him to a position of authority in Egypt (Genesis 37-50), setbacks can catalyze creative thinking and the exploration of uncharted territories.

3. Building Tenacity

James 1:12 (NIV) encourages perseverance: "Blessed is the one who perseveres under trial because, having stood the test, that person will receive the crown of life that the Lord has promised to those who love him." Setbacks test our resolve and determination. By persevering through challenges, we build inner strength and tenacity.

4. Strengthening Character

The process of overcoming setbacks shapes our character, fostering qualities such as patience, resilience, and determination. Romans 5:3-4 (NIV) emphasizes this growth: "Not only so, but we also glory in our sufferings, because we know that suffering produces perseverance; perseverance, character; and character, hope."

Conclusion

Learning from failure and turning setbacks into opportunities is a transformative journey that requires courage, resilience, and a willingness to embrace change. By gleaning lessons from failures, humbly adapting to challenges, reframing setbacks as stepping stones, and fostering creativity and tenacity, individuals can harness the power of setbacks to propel themselves toward greater success and personal fulfillment. Through these processes, they not only develop as individuals but also deepen their faith, character, and capacity to overcome life's obstacles. Just as a seed germinates in darkness to eventually flourish, setbacks can serve as the fertile ground from which new opportunities and growth emerge.

Learning from Failure and Turning Setbacks into Opportunities: Biblical Wisdom for Growth and Transformation

Failure and setbacks are integral parts of the human experience, yet they possess the potential to become powerful catalysts for growth, resilience, and transformation. By adopting a biblical perspective and drawing on the wisdom of Scripture, we can navigate the challenges of failure and setbacks with a mindset focused on learning, redemption, and the realization of newfound opportunities.

Learning from Failure

1. Embracing Humility

Proverbs 16:18 (NIV) reminds us of the dangers of pride: "Pride goes before destruction, a haughty spirit before a fall." Failure humbles us and prompts us to acknowledge our limitations. This humility opens the door to self-awareness and a willingness to learn from our mistakes.

2. Perseverance through Trials

James 1:2-4 (NIV) underscores the value of perseverance amid trials: "Consider it pure joy, my brothers and sisters, whenever you face trials of many kinds, because you know that the testing of your faith produces perseverance. Let perseverance finish its work so that you may be mature and complete, not lacking anything." Failure can serve as a refining process that develops perseverance and ultimately leads to maturity.

3. Seeking God's Wisdom

Proverbs 3:5-6 (NIV) offers guidance for seeking divine wisdom in times of uncertainty: "Trust in the Lord with all your heart and lean not on your own understanding; in all your ways submit to him, and he will make your paths straight." Failure prompts us to turn to God for guidance and wisdom, recognizing that His perspective far surpasses our own.

Turning Setbacks into Opportunities

1. God's Redemptive Power

Romans 8:28 (NIV) assures us of God's redemptive power in all circumstances: "And we know that in all things God works for the good of those who love him, who have been called according to his purpose." Even in the midst of setbacks, God can work to bring about greater good and fulfill His purpose in our lives.

2. Transformation through Renewal

Romans 12:2 (NIV) speaks of transformation through renewal of the mind: "Do not conform to the pattern of this world, but be transformed by the renewing of your mind. Then you will be able to test and approve what God's will is—his good, pleasing and perfect will." Setbacks provide opportunities for a renewed perspective, allowing us to align our thoughts with God's will.

3. Perseverance and Hope

2 Corinthians 4:8-9 (NIV) illustrates the potential for endurance and hope through trials: "We are hard pressed on every side, but not crushed; perplexed, but not in despair; persecuted, but not abandoned; struck down, but not destroyed." Setbacks can foster perseverance and instill a sense of hope that transcends challenging circumstances.

4. God's Promise of Restoration

Joel 2:25-26 (NIV) speaks of God's promise of restoration: "I will repay you for the years the locusts have eaten—the great locust and the young locust, the other locusts and the locust swarm—my great army that I sent among you. You will have plenty to eat, until you are full, and you will praise the name of the Lord your God, who has worked wonders for you." Even in times of setback, God's promise of restoration and abundance remains.

Conclusion

Learning from failure and turning setbacks into opportunities is a transformative process that aligns with the teachings of Scripture. By embracing humility, seeking God's wisdom, persevering through trials, and trusting in His redemptive power, we can navigate the challenges of failure with faith and hope. Setbacks, when approached with a biblical perspective, can lead to growth, resilience, and the discovery of new doors that God opens for us. Just as the Apostle Paul found strength in his weaknesses (2 Corinthians 12:9), we too can find strength in our setbacks and emerge as vessels of God's grace and transformation.

6.3 The importance of adaptability and flexibility

The Importance of Adaptability and Flexibility: Thriving in an Ever-Changing World

In an ever-evolving world characterized by rapid technological advancements, shifting economic landscapes, and unforeseen challenges, the virtues of adaptability and flexibility have emerged as crucial qualities for personal and professional success. These attributes enable individuals to navigate uncertainty, seize opportunities, and maintain a resilient spirit. By embracing adaptability and flexibility, individuals can not only thrive in the face of change but also become catalysts for growth, innovation, and positive transformation.

Embracing Change with Adaptability

1. Navigating Uncertainty

Change is an inevitable aspect of life, and adaptability equips individuals with the ability to navigate uncertain terrain with grace and composure. Proverbs 3:5-6 (NIV) provides guidance: "Trust in the Lord with all your heart and lean not on your own understanding; in all your ways submit to him, and he will make your paths straight." Embracing change requires a trustful reliance on God's guidance, allowing us to confidently chart new paths even in unfamiliar territories.

2. Embracing Lifelong Learning

Adaptability encourages a mindset of continuous learning and growth. Proverbs 18:15 (NIV) asserts, "The heart of the discerning acquires knowledge, for the ears of the wise seek it out." Those who cultivate a hunger for knowledge and eagerly embrace new skills position themselves for ongoing development and relevance in an ever-changing world.

3. Fostering Resilience

Adaptability builds resilience—the ability to bounce back from setbacks and maintain a positive outlook. James 1:12 (NIV) speaks of the blessings that await those who persevere: "Blessed is the one who perseveres under trial because, having stood the test, that person will receive the crown of life that the Lord has promised to those who love him." Resilience enables individuals to confront challenges head-on, drawing strength from their ability to adapt to shifting circumstances.

Embracing Opportunities with Flexibility

1. Seizing New Opportunities

Flexibility enables individuals to seize unexpected opportunities that may arise. Proverbs 16:9 (NIV) assures us, "In their hearts humans plan their course, but the Lord establishes their steps." Remaining open to detours and unexpected turns allows us to recognize and capitalize on new doors that God may open along the way.

2. Innovation and Creativity

Flexibility nurtures innovation by encouraging individuals to approach problems from different angles and explore unconventional solutions. Romans 12:2 (NIV) encourages transformative thinking: "Do not conform to the pattern of this world, but be transformed by the renewing of your mind. Then you will be able to test and approve what God's will is—his good, pleasing and perfect will." Flexibility allows us to break free from rigid patterns and discover innovative ways to address challenges.

3. Enhancing Relationships

Flexibility enhances interpersonal relationships by fostering understanding and adaptability in various social contexts. Philippians 2:3-4 (NIV) highlights the importance of humility and considering others: "Do nothing out of selfish ambition or vain conceit. Rather, in humility value others above yourselves, not looking to your own interests but each of you to the interests of the others." Flexibility allows us to accommodate diverse perspectives and collaborate effectively.

Conclusion

Adaptability and flexibility are essential virtues that empower individuals to navigate the complexities of an ever-changing world. By embracing change, cultivating resilience, and maintaining a lifelong learning mindset, individuals can navigate uncertainty with confidence. Simultaneously, by staying open to new opportunities, fostering innovation, and enhancing relationships, flexibility enables individuals to capitalize on the dynamic nature of their surroundings.

As we embrace these qualities, we align ourselves with biblical principles that encourage trust in God's guidance, perseverance through trials, and a humble willingness to adapt. Just as a well-rooted tree sways with the wind while remaining firmly planted, individuals who prioritize adaptability and flexibility stand poised to weather life's storms while flourishing and bearing fruit. These virtues not only contribute to personal success but also enable us to make meaningful contributions to the world, driving positive change, and glorifying God in all we do.

6.4 Embracing continuous learning and personal growth.

Embracing Continuous Learning and Personal Growth: Unleashing Your Potential

In a world characterized by rapid technological advancements, shifting paradigms, and evolving knowledge, the pursuit of continuous learning and personal growth has become paramount. Embracing this journey is a transformative endeavor that not only equips individuals with the skills and knowledge needed to thrive but also nurtures a mindset of curiosity, adaptability, and resilience.

The Essence of Continuous Learning

1. Lifelong Relevance

Continuous learning transcends the boundaries of age, occupation, or background, ensuring that individuals remain relevant and adaptable in an ever-changing landscape. Proverbs 18:15 (NIV) captures this sentiment: "The heart of the discerning acquires knowledge, for the ears of the wise seek it out." A commitment to ongoing learning empowers individuals to stay informed and make informed decisions.

2. Expanding Horizons

The pursuit of knowledge broadens horizons and deepens understanding. Proverbs 1:5 (NIV) underscores the value of knowledge: "Let the wise listen and add to their learning, and let the discerning get guidance." By continuously seeking new insights, individuals gain a holistic perspective that enables them to make well-rounded judgments.

3. Fostering Innovation

Continuous learning fuels innovation by encouraging individuals to think critically and creatively. Romans 12:2 (NIV) emphasizes transformative thinking: "Do not conform to the pattern of this world, but be transformed by the renewing of your mind. Then you will be able to test and approve what God's will is—his good, pleasing and perfect will." A commitment to personal growth fosters the ability to approach challenges from fresh angles and devise innovative solutions.

The Path of Personal Growth

1. Unleashing Potential

Personal growth is a journey of unlocking one's full potential and becoming the best version of oneself. Jeremiah 29:11 (NIV) encapsulates God's plan for our lives: "For I know the plans I have for you, plans to prosper you and not to harm you, plans to give you hope and a future." Embracing personal growth aligns with God's desire for us to flourish and fulfill His purpose for our lives.

2. Building Resilience

Personal growth is intertwined with resilience—the ability to bounce back from setbacks and thrive in adversity. James 1:2-4 (NIV) speaks of the benefits of perseverance: "Consider it pure joy, my brothers and sisters, whenever you face trials of many kinds, because you know that the testing of your faith produces perseverance. Let perseverance finish its work so that you may be mature and complete, not lacking anything." Through challenges, we develop character, resilience, and a deeper reliance on God.

3. Contributing to Others

Personal growth equips individuals to contribute meaningfully to the lives of others. Philippians 2:3-4 (NIV) emphasizes humility and considering others' interests: "Do nothing out of selfish ambition or vain conceit. Rather, in humility value others above yourselves, not looking to your own interests but each of you to the interests of the others." By developing our strengths and character, we are better positioned to impact our communities and share our gifts with the world.

Conclusion

Embracing continuous learning and personal growth is a journey that intertwines the pursuit of knowledge with the cultivation of character. As we seek wisdom, expand our horizons, and foster innovation, we honor God's call to steward our minds and abilities. Simultaneously, the path of personal growth empowers us to unleash our potential, weather life's storms with resilience, and make a positive impact on others.

By nurturing these qualities, we align ourselves with biblical principles that encourage us to seek wisdom, grow in faith, and develop a servant's heart. Just as a tree grows taller, stronger, and more fruitful with time, individuals committed to continuous learning and personal growth stand poised to reach new heights, contribute meaningfully to the world, and glorify God through their journey of becoming.

CHAPTER SEVEN
CULTIVATING A POSITIVE MINDSET

Cultivating a Positive Mindset

Cultivating a Positive Mindset: Nurturing Inner Resilience and Joy

A positive mindset is a powerful force that shapes our perception of the world, influences our reactions to challenges, and ultimately impacts our overall well-being. It involves cultivating an optimistic outlook, focusing on the silver linings, and embracing a mindset of gratitude cond hope. Nurturing a positive mindset is not only beneficial for our mental and emotional health but also plays a pivotal role in shaping our interactions with others and our ability to navigate life's ups and downs.

The Foundations of a Positive Mindset

1. Gratitude and Contentment

Philippians 4:6-7 (NIV) guides us in cultivating gratitude: "Do not be anxious about anything, but in every situation, by prayer and petition, with thanksgiving, present your requests to God. And the peace of God, which transcends all understanding, will guard your hearts and your minds in Christ Jesus." Gratitude redirects our focus from what we lack to the blessings we have, fostering contentment and inner peace.

2. Renewing the Mind

Romans 12:2 (NIV) underscores the importance of transforming our minds: "Do not conform to the pattern of this world, but be transformed by the renewing of your mind. Then you will be able to test and approve what God's will is—his good, pleasing and perfect will." Cultivating a positive mindset involves intentionally replacing negative thought patterns with thoughts that align with God's truth and promises.

3. Letting Go of Negativity

Ephesians 4:31-32 (NIV) encourages us to rid ourselves of negative emotions: "Get rid of all bitterness, rage and anger, brawling and slander, along with every form of malice. Be kind and compassionate to one another, forgiving each other, just as in Christ God forgave you." Letting go of negativity allows space for positivity to flourish, fostering a healthier mental and emotional state.

Navigating Challenges with a Positive Perspective

1. Resilience in Adversity

James 1:2-4 (NIV) speaks of the role of trials in shaping our character: "Consider it pure joy, my brothers and sisters, whenever you face trials of many kinds, because you know that the testing of your faith produces perseverance. Let perseverance finish its work so that you may be mature and complete, not lacking anything." A positive mindset enables us to approach challenges with resilience, viewing them as opportunities for growth.

2. Focusing on Solutions

A positive mindset empowers us to approach problems with a solution-oriented mindset. Rather than dwelling on obstacles, we channel our energy into finding creative and constructive ways to overcome them. Philippians 4:13 (NIV) resonates with this perspective: "I can do all this through him who gives me strength."

3. Empowering Relationships

Proverbs 17:22 (NIV) highlights the impact of a joyful heart: "A cheerful heart is good medicine, but a crushed spirit dries up the bones." A positive mindset not only benefits us individually but also enhances our relationships. By radiating positivity, we uplift those around us, fostering an environment of encouragement and support.

Conclusion

Cultivating a positive mindset is a transformative journey that requires intentionality, self-awareness, and alignment with biblical principles. By embracing gratitude, renewing our minds, and letting go of negativity, we create space for joy, peace, and resilience to flourish within us. This positive perspective equips us to navigate life's challenges with grace, view setbacks as stepping stones, and inspire others through our example. As we embrace a positive mindset, we align ourselves with God's desire for us to experience abundant life and reflect His light in a world that needs hope and encouragement.

7.1 The power of gratitude and positive affirmations

The Power of Gratitude and Positive Affirmations: Transforming Mindsets and Cultivating Abundance

In a world often consumed by stress, negativity, and uncertainty, the practices of gratitude and positive affirmations stand as beacons of light, offering transformative power to shape our thoughts, emotions, and actions. These practices are rooted in the belief that our minds are malleable, and by intentionally directing our focus toward the positive, we can create profound shifts in our outlook on life and our overall well-being. As we explore the depths of gratitude and the potency of positive affirmations, we embark on a journey of self-discovery, inner transformation, and the cultivation of abundance in our lives.

The Essence of Gratitude

Gratitude, a fundamental virtue in various cultures and religions, involves recognizing and appreciating the blessings, experiences, and relationships that enrich our lives. It goes beyond a mere thank-you; it's a heart-centered practice that fosters a deep sense of contentment, joy, and connection.

1. Shifting Perspective

Gratitude prompts us to shift our perspective from what we lack to what we have. Philippians 4:6-7 (NIV) encapsulates this shift: "Do not be anxious about anything, but in every situation, by prayer and petition, with thanksgiving, present your requests to God. And the peace of God, which transcends all understanding, will guard your hearts and your minds in Christ Jesus." By focusing on the positive aspects of our lives, we invite God's peace to reign in our hearts.

2. Cultivating Resilience

Gratitude enhances resilience by teaching us to find silver linings even in challenging situations. Romans 8:28 (NIV) assures us of God's transformative power in all circumstances: "And we know that in all things God works for the good of those who love him, who have been called according to his purpose." Gratitude empowers us to view setbacks as opportunities for growth and transformation.

3. Strengthening Relationships

Gratitude deepens our relationships by fostering kindness, empathy, and a spirit of giving. Ephesians 4:32 (NIV) guides us: "Be kind and compassionate to one another, forgiving each other, just as in Christ God forgave you." Expressing gratitude toward others not only strengthens bonds but also reflects Christ's love and selflessness.

The Power of Positive Affirmations

Positive affirmations are statements of self-empowerment and encouragement that are intentionally repeated to influence our thoughts and beliefs. They operate on the principle that our minds are receptive to the messages we feed them, and by affirming positive truths, we can reshape our self-perception and reality.

1. Rewriting Inner Dialogue

Positive affirmations counter negative self-talk and limiting beliefs. Romans 12:2 (NIV) emphasizes transformation through mind renewal: "Do not conform to the pattern of this world, but be transformed by the renewing of your mind. Then you will be able to test and approve what God's will is—his good, pleasing and perfect will." Affirmations enable us to replace self-doubt with confidence, aligning our thoughts with God's truth.

2. Enhancing Self-Confidence

Affirmations boost self-confidence and self-worth. Psalm 139:14 (NIV) celebrates God's creation: "I praise you because I am fearfully and wonderfully made; your works are wonderful; I know that full well." Affirmations remind us of our inherent value as God's creation, empowering us to approach life with self-assuredness.

3. Manifesting Positivity

Positive affirmations have the power to shape our reality. Mark 11:23 (NIV) speaks to the potential of faith: "Truly I tell you, if anyone says to this mountain, 'Go, throw yourself into the sea,' and does not doubt in their heart but believes that what they say will happen, it will be done for them." By affirming positive outcomes, we align our thoughts with our desired reality and invite God's hand to work in our lives.

Creating a Synergy

Gratitude and positive affirmations complement each other, creating a synergy that magnifies their impact. Gratitude serves as a foundation of humility and openness, while positive affirmations infuse empowerment and intentionality.

1. Gratitude Amplifies Affirmations

Gratitude enhances the effectiveness of positive affirmations by attuning our hearts to receive and appreciate the blessings we affirm. Psalm 118:24 (NIV) celebrates each day as a gift: "This is the day the Lord has made; let us rejoice and be glad in it." When we affirm positive truths, our grateful hearts become fertile ground for their manifestation.

2. Affirmations Deepen Gratitude

Positive affirmations deepen our sense of gratitude by reminding us of God's promises and our inherent worth. 1 Thessalonians 5:18 (NIV) exhorts us to give thanks in all circumstances: "Give thanks in all circumstances; for this is God's will for you in Christ Jesus." Affirmations reinforce our appreciation for God's goodness and faithfulness.

Wherefore, the power of gratitude and positive affirmations lies in their ability to shape our inner world and influence our external reality. By embracing gratitude, we shift our focus from lack to abundance, fostering resilience and nurturing relationships. Positive affirmations, in turn, rewrite our internal narrative, boosting self-confidence and inviting positive outcomes. When these practices intertwine, they create a harmonious symphony of transformation, enabling us to cultivate an empowered mindset, experience greater joy, and navigate life's challenges with unwavering faith.

Through gratitude and positive affirmations, we tap into God's boundless grace, aligning our hearts and minds with His truth. As we immerse ourselves in these transformative practices, we not only enhance our personal well-being but also radiate positivity and love, impacting those around us and glorifying the Creator who offers us an abundance of blessings and hope.

7.2 Visualizing success and creating a compelling vision

Visualizing Success and Creating a Compelling Vision: Unlocking the Power of Imagination and Purpose

Visualizing success and creating a compelling vision are dynamic practices that harness the creative power of the mind to shape our future, drive motivation, and bring our aspirations to life. Rooted in the principles of imagination and intention, these practices empower individuals to bridge the gap between their current reality and their desired outcomes. By delving into the depths of visualization and vision creation, we embark on a transformative journey that ignites passion, propels action, and leads to the realization of our deepest aspirations.

The Art of Visualization

1. The Power of Imagination

Imagination is a divine gift that enables us to create mental images, scenarios, and experiences that extend beyond our immediate surroundings. Proverbs 29:18 (NIV) highlights the significance of vision: "Where there is no revelation, people cast off restraint; but blessed is the one who heeds wisdom's instruction." Visualization serves as a form of revelation, allowing us to see possibilities and potentials that guide our actions.

2. The Science of Visualization

Scientific research supports the efficacy of visualization in achieving goals. Visualization activates neural pathways in the brain, priming the mind and body for success. Philippians 4:13 (NIV) resonates with this concept: "I can do all this through him who gives me strength." Visualization aligns our thoughts and emotions with the belief that we can overcome obstacles and achieve our aspirations.

3. Creating a Mental Blueprint

Visualization involves crafting a mental blueprint of the desired outcome. Just as God instructed Noah to build the ark according to a specific plan (Genesis 6:15), we construct our visions with attention to detail. By vividly imagining the journey toward success, we provide our minds with a roadmap to follow.

Crafting a Compelling Vision

1. Aligning with Purpose

A compelling vision is rooted in purpose and aligned with one's values and calling. Proverbs 20:5 (NIV) speaks to the depths of the heart's counsel: "The purposes of a person's heart are deep waters, but one who has insight draws them out." A well-crafted vision taps into the depths of our heart's desires and illuminates our path forward.

2. Envisioning the Impact

A compelling vision extends beyond personal achievement to encompass the greater impact on oneself and others. Proverbs 11:25

(NIV) emphasizes generosity: "A generous person will prosper; whoever refreshes others will be refreshed." A vision that positively impacts others not only brings fulfillment but also aligns with God's call to serve and uplift.

3. Setting Clear Goals

A compelling vision is underpinned by clear, actionable goals. Habakkuk 2:2-3 (NIV) speaks of the importance of clear vision: "Write down the revelation and make it plain on tablets so that a herald may run with it. For the revelation awaits an appointed time; it speaks of the end and will not prove false." Setting specific goals provides a tangible framework for turning vision into reality.

Unleashing the Synergy

The practice of visualizing success and creating a compelling vision forms a powerful synergy that amplifies their impact.

1. Energizing Intentions

Visualization infuses a compelling vision with energy and enthusiasm. Romans 12:11 (NIV) speaks of zeal: "Never be lacking in zeal, but keep your spiritual fervor, serving the Lord." Visualization infuses our vision with the passion and drive needed to pursue it with fervor.

2. Amplifying Focus

A compelling vision sharpens the focus of visualization. Hebrews 12:2 (NIV) encourages us to fix our eyes on Jesus: "Fixing our eyes on Jesus, the pioneer and perfecter of faith." A well-defined vision provides a specific target for visualization, enhancing its effectiveness.

3. Inspiring Action

Together, visualization and a compelling vision inspire intentional action. James 2:17 (NIV) speaks of faith and deeds: "In the same way, faith by itself, if it is not accompanied by action, is dead." By consistently visualizing success and aligning our actions with our vision, we breathe life into our aspirations.

Conclusion

Visualizing success and creating a compelling vision are dynamic practices that tap into the boundless potential of the human mind and spirit. By harnessing the power of imagination, intention, and purpose, individuals can bridge the gap between their present reality and their desired future. As we visualize success and craft compelling visions, we align ourselves with divine principles that emphasize the importance of faith, intention, and purposeful action.

Incorporating these practices into our lives not only propels us toward our goals but also invites God's guidance and blessings. Through the art of visualization and the creation of a compelling vision, we actively participate in shaping our destiny, transforming our inner world, and realizing our potential. Just as God breathed life into creation (Genesis 2:7), we, too, can breathe life into our dreams, infusing them with intention, purpose, and unwavering faith. As we embark on this transformative journey, we invite the divine to partner with our efforts, leading us toward a future marked by achievement, fulfillment, and the abundant realization of God's blessings.

7.3 Developing a resilience mindset through affirmations

Developing a Resilience Mindset Through Affirmations: Embracing Strength, Faith, and Hope

In a world often characterized by challenges, setbacks, and uncertainties, the practice of developing a resilience mindset through affirmations emerges as a powerful tool for cultivating inner strength, unwavering faith, and enduring hope. Rooted in the principles of positive psychology and grounded in biblical truths, affirmations serve as a transformative practice that empowers individuals to navigate adversity with grace, bounce back from setbacks, and emerge stronger than before. As we explore the depths of resilience mindset development through affirmations, we embark on a journey of self-discovery, spiritual growth, and the unwavering belief in God's guiding hand.

Understanding Resilience Mindset

1. The Foundation of Resilience

Resilience is the ability to bounce back, adapt, and thrive in the face of adversity. It involves cultivating a mindset that embraces challenges as opportunities for growth and transformation. James 1:2-4 (NIV) captures the essence of resilience: "Consider it pure joy, my brothers and sisters, whenever you face trials of many kinds, because you know that the testing of your faith produces perseverance. Let perseverance finish its work so that you may be mature and complete, not lacking anything." Resilience mindset encourages us to view challenges as refining experiences that shape our character.

2. The Power of Affirmations

Affirmations are positive statements that are intentionally repeated to influence our thoughts and beliefs. They serve as a form of self-talk that reinforces positive thinking patterns and shapes our perception of ourselves and the world around us. Proverbs 18:21 (NIV) highlights the significance of our words: "The tongue has the power of life and death, and those who love it will eat its fruit." Affirmations, when rooted in biblical truth, can breathe life into our thoughts and emotions.

Developing a Resilience Mindset Through Affirmations

1. Embracing God's Strength

Affirmations centered on God's strength infuse us with the assurance that we can overcome challenges with His help. Philippians 4:13 (NIV) reinforces this truth: "I can do all this through him who gives me strength." Affirmations such as "I am strong in the Lord and His power sustains me" empower us to rely on divine strength in times of difficulty.

2. Trusting God's Sovereignty

Affirmations that emphasize trust in God's sovereignty remind us that He is in control, even in the midst of challenges. Proverbs 3:5-6 (NIV) guides our trust: "Trust in the Lord with all your heart and lean not on your own understanding; in all your ways submit to him, and he will make your paths straight." Affirmations like "I trust God's plan for my life, even when things are tough" anchor us in the belief that God is working all things together for good.

3. Cultivating Enduring Faith

Affirmations that nurture faith remind us of God's faithfulness and encourage us to persevere. Hebrews 11:1 (NIV) defines faith: "Now faith is confidence in what we hope for and assurance about what we do not see." Affirmations such as "I have unwavering faith in God's promises, even in adversity" inspire us to hold onto hope and stand firm in our convictions.

4. Overcoming Fear and Doubt

Affirmations that counter fear and doubt with God's truth empower us to rise above negative emotions. 2 Timothy 1:7 (NIV) speaks to the power of a sound mind: "For the Spirit God gave us does not make us timid, but gives us power, love and self-discipline." Affirmations like "I am courageous and capable of facing any challenge with God by my side" equip us to confront fear with faith.

5. Finding Joy in Adversity

Affirmations that focus on finding joy in adversity redirect our perspective toward gratitude and resilience. 1 Thessalonians 5:18 (NIV) exhorts us: "Give thanks in all circumstances; for this is God's will for you in Christ Jesus." Affirmations such as "I find joy in every situation, knowing that God's grace is sufficient for me" help us see trials as opportunities for spiritual growth.

6. Embracing God's Peace

Affirmations centered on God's peace remind us to seek His tranquility amidst life's challenges. Philippians 4:7 (NIV) promises: "And the peace of God, which transcends all understanding, will guard your hearts and your minds in Christ Jesus." Affirmations like "I am anchored in God's peace that surpasses all understanding" enable us to experience inner calmness in turbulent times.

7. Walking in Purpose

Affirmations that affirm our purpose remind us that our challenges contribute to a greater plan. Jeremiah 29:11 (NIV) speaks to God's purpose: "For I know the plans I have for you, plans to prosper you and not to harm you, plans to give you hope and a future." Affirmations such as "I am fulfilling God's purpose for my life, even through challenges" give us a sense of direction and meaning.

Conclusion

Developing a resilience mindset through affirmations is a transformative practice that aligns our thoughts, emotions, and beliefs with God's truth. By intentionally directing our focus toward positive, empowering statements rooted in biblical principles, we shape our perception of challenges, setbacks, and uncertainties. As we anchor our affirmations in God's promises, we cultivate a mindset of strength, faith, and hope that enables us to navigate adversity with unwavering resolve.

Affirmations serve as a spiritual discipline that empowers us to overcome fear, doubt, and negativity while nurturing virtues of trust, perseverance, and joy. Through the synergy of affirmations and a resilience mindset, we not only weather life's storms with grace but also emerge from them transformed, strengthened, and closer to God's purpose for our lives. As we declare and internalize these affirmations, we embrace the fullness of God's guidance, protection, and provision, allowing His truth to shape our identity and sustain us on our journey of resilience and spiritual growth.

7.4 Nurturing optimism and reframing failure as feedback

Nurturing Optimism and Reframing Failure as Feedback: A Path to Growth and Resilience

In the tapestry of human experience, optimism and the art of reframing failure as feedback are powerful threads that weave together resilience, personal growth, and a vibrant outlook on life. Rooted in the principles of positive psychology and grounded in the wisdom of learning from setbacks, these practices offer transformative ways to approach challenges, setbacks, and the complexities of existence. As we delve into the realms of nurturing optimism and embracing failure as a constructive force, we embark on a journey that empowers us to cultivate a mindset of strength, wisdom, and unwavering hope.

Nurturing Optimism

1. The Essence of Optimism

Optimism is a lens through which we view the world with a hopeful, positive perspective. It's not about denying the existence of difficulties but rather about approaching them with a belief that positive outcomes are possible. Romans 15:13 (NIV) captures the essence of hope: "May the God of hope fill you with all joy and peace as you trust in him, so that you may overflow with hope by the power of the Holy Spirit." Optimism aligns with the biblical call to trust in God's goodness and promises.

2. Cultivating Positive Thinking

Nurturing optimism involves consciously cultivating positive thoughts and attitudes. Philippians 4:8 (NIV) guides our thought life: "Finally, brothers and sisters, whatever is true, whatever is noble, whatever is right, whatever is pure, whatever is lovely, whatever is admirable—if anything is excellent or praiseworthy—think about such things." Optimism encourages us to focus on the positive aspects of situations, fostering a mindset of gratitude and joy.

3. Embracing Resilience

Optimism and resilience are intertwined, as an optimistic outlook fuels our ability to bounce back from adversity. James 1:12 (NIV) speaks to the rewards of perseverance: "Blessed is the one who perseveres under trial because, having stood the test, that person will receive the crown of life that the Lord has promised to those who love him." Optimism empowers us to view challenges as opportunities for growth and perseverance.

Reframing Failure as Feedback

1. Rethinking Failure

Reframing failure as feedback involves shifting our perspective on failure from a final outcome to a stepping stone in the journey of growth. Proverbs 24:16 (NIV) speaks of resilience in adversity: "for though the righteous fall seven times, they rise again, but the wicked stumble when calamity strikes." Embracing failure as feedback enables us to rise again and continue moving forward.

2. Extracting Lessons

Failure provides valuable insights and lessons that guide us toward improvement. Proverbs 2:6 (NIV) highlights the role of wisdom: "For the Lord gives wisdom; from his mouth come knowledge and understanding." Viewing failure as feedback prompts us to seek wisdom from our experiences, refining our approach and decision-making.

3. Building Character

Reframing failure as feedback contributes to the development of character and resilience. Romans 5:3-4 (NIV) speaks of perseverance leading to character: "Not only so, but we also glory in our sufferings, because we know that suffering produces perseverance; perseverance, character; and character, hope." Failure, when seen as a source of feedback, becomes a catalyst for character-building and growth.

4. Fostering Innovation

Failure encourages innovation and creativity as we explore alternative paths. Isaiah 43:19 (NIV) speaks of God's transformative work: "See, I am doing a new thing! Now it springs up; do you not perceive it?" Reframing failure as feedback opens us to new possibilities and ideas, enabling us to adapt and innovate.

5. Strengthening Determination

Reframing failure as feedback bolsters our determination to succeed. Galatians 6:9 (NIV) encourages persistence: "Let us not become weary in doing good, for at the proper time we will reap a harvest if we do not give up." When we view failure as feedback, we are motivated to persevere, knowing that each setback brings us closer to success.

Conclusion

Nurturing optimism and reframing failure as feedback are transformative practices that shape our perspective, drive our actions, and empower us to embrace the challenges of life with hope and resilience. By fostering an optimistic outlook, we align ourselves with God's promise of joy, peace, and a future filled with His goodness. Likewise, by viewing failure as feedback, we tap into the wellspring of wisdom, character-building, and innovation that emerges from setbacks.

Through the synergy of these practices, we cultivate a mindset that embraces challenges as opportunities, and setbacks as stepping stones toward growth. As we journey through life, may we continuously nurture optimism in our hearts and approach failure with the wisdom to extract its valuable lessons. By aligning our thoughts and actions with these transformative principles, we become living testimonies of God's grace, resilience, and the incredible capacity for growth and renewal that resides within us.

CHAPTER EIGHT
DEVELOPING SUPPORTIVE HABITS

Developing Supportive Habits

Developing Supportive Habits: Nurturing a Foundation for Success and Well-being

Habits, those subtle yet powerful patterns of behavior, shape the trajectory of our lives. From our physical health to our mental well-being, from personal growth to spiritual development, the habits we cultivate play a significant role in shaping who we are and who we become. In this exploration of developing supportive habits, we delve into the intricacies of how intentional choices and consistent practices can create a solid foundation for success, resilience, and a life aligned with biblical principles.

Understanding Habits

1. The Nature of Habits

Habits are automatic behaviors that are formed through repetition. They can be either supportive, contributing positively to our well-being, or detrimental, hindering our progress. Romans 12:2 (NIV) emphasizes the transformative power of renewing our minds: "Do not conform to the pattern of this world, but be transformed by the renewing of your mind. Then you will be able to test and approve what God's will is—his good, pleasing and perfect will." Supportive habits align with God's will and contribute to our transformation.

2. The Habit Loop

Habits consist of a loop: cue, routine, and reward. By identifying triggers (cues) and intentionally choosing positive behaviors (routines) that lead to desirable outcomes (rewards), we can intentionally shape our habits. Philippians 4:8 (NIV) guides our focus: "Finally, brothers and sisters, whatever is true, whatever is noble, whatever is right, whatever is pure, whatever is lovely, whatever is admirable—if anything is excellent or praiseworthy—think about such things." Habits rooted in positive thoughts align with this call.

Developing Supportive Habits

1. Habit of Gratitude

Cultivating a habit of gratitude involves regularly expressing thankfulness for blessings. 1 Thessalonians 5:18 (NIV) exhorts us: "Give thanks in all circumstances; for this is God's will for you in Christ Jesus." By practicing gratitude, we shift our focus toward the positive aspects of life, fostering joy and contentment.

2. Habit of Daily Reflection

Regular reflection encourages self-awareness and personal growth. Psalm 139:23-24 (NIV) guides introspection: "Search me, God, and know my heart; test me and know my anxious thoughts. See if there is any offensive way in me, and lead me in the way everlasting." Developing a habit of reflection aligns with seeking God's guidance for continuous improvement.

3. Habit of Physical Exercise

Physical exercise promotes overall well-being. 1 Corinthians 6:19-20 (NIV) underscores the body's significance: "Do you not know that your bodies are temples of the Holy Spirit, who is in you, whom you have received from God? You are not your own; you were bought at a price. Therefore, honor God with your bodies." Cultivating a habit of regular exercise honors the stewardship of our bodies.

4. Habit of Mindful Eating

Mindful eating involves being present during meals and making intentional food choices. 1 Corinthians 10:31 (NIV) emphasizes honoring God in all aspects of life: "So whether you eat or drink or whatever you do, do it all for the glory of God." Developing a habit of mindful eating aligns with the principle of stewardship and honoring God through our choices.

5. Habit of Rest and Sabbath

Taking regular rest and observing a Sabbath promotes spiritual and emotional well-being. Matthew 11:28-30 (NIV) speaks of finding rest in Christ: "Come to me, all you who are weary and burdened, and I will give you rest. Take my yoke upon you and learn from me, for I am gentle and humble in heart, and you will find rest for your souls. For my yoke is easy and my burden is light." Cultivating a habit of rest reflects our trust in God's provision and care.

6. Habit of Prayer and Meditation

Regular prayer and meditation nurture spiritual growth and connection with God. Philippians 4:6-7 (NIV) encourages prayer and peace: "Do not be anxious about anything, but in every situation, by prayer and petition, with thanksgiving, present your requests to God. And the peace of God, which transcends all understanding, will guard your hearts and your minds in Christ Jesus." Developing a habit of prayer and meditation deepens our relationship with God.

7. Habit of Lifelong Learning

Cultivating a habit of continuous learning promotes personal and intellectual growth. Proverbs 18:15 (NIV) extols the value of seeking knowledge: "The heart of the discerning acquires knowledge, for the ears of the wise seek it out." By embracing a habit of learning, we honor God's gift of curiosity and pursue excellence in all areas of life.

8. Habit of Acts of Kindness

Practicing acts of kindness contributes to a culture of compassion and empathy. Ephesians 4:32 (NIV) guides our interactions: "Be kind and compassionate to one another, forgiving each other, just as in Christ God forgave you." Developing a habit of kindness reflects Christ's love and extends grace to others.

Conclusion

Developing supportive habits is a deliberate and transformative process that empowers us to align our actions with our values and aspirations. By intentionally cultivating habits rooted in gratitude, reflection, self-care, and spiritual growth, we create a foundation for success, resilience, and well-being. As we practice these habits, we honor God's design for abundant living and reflect His principles in our daily lives.

The journey of developing supportive habits is not about perfection but about progress. It's a journey that invites us to continually seek growth, embrace change, and draw closer to God's purposes for our lives. By anchoring our habits in biblical truths, we navigate life's challenges with grace, cultivate resilience, and shine as beacons of light and love in a world that yearns for positive transformation.

8.1 The role of discipline and consistency

The Role of Discipline and Consistency: Nurturing Growth, Achieving Excellence, and Honoring God's Design

Discipline and consistency are twin pillars that form the foundation of success, character development, and a life that reflects God's wisdom and purpose. Rooted in principles of self-control, commitment, and diligence, these virtues guide us on a transformative journey of growth, personal development, and spiritual alignment. In this exploration, we delve into the profound role of discipline and consistency, drawing wisdom from both biblical teachings and practical insights.

Understanding Discipline and Consistency

1. The Essence of Discipline

Discipline is the practice of self-control and adherence to principles, even in the face of challenges or distractions. Proverbs 25:28 (NIV) speaks to the importance of self-control: "Like a city whose walls are broken through is a person who lacks self-control." Discipline involves setting boundaries and making intentional choices that align with our goals and values.

2. The Power of Consistency

Consistency is the act of faithfully repeating actions over time, allowing them to accumulate into meaningful results. Galatians 6:9 (NIV) encourages perseverance: "Let us not become weary in doing good, for at the proper time we will reap a harvest if we do not give up." Consistency empowers us to overcome challenges and realize the fruits of our efforts.

The Synergy of Discipline and Consistency

1. A Recipe for Excellence

Discipline and consistency form the recipe for achieving excellence in any endeavor. Colossians 3:23-24 (NIV) emphasizes excellence in service: "Whatever you do, work at it with all your heart, as working for the Lord, not for human masters, since you know that you will receive an inheritance from the Lord as a reward." The combination of disciplined effort and unwavering consistency propels us toward excellence.

2. Character Building

Discipline and consistency contribute to the development of character and integrity. Proverbs 10:4 (NIV) underscores diligence: "Lazy hands make for poverty, but diligent hands bring wealth." The disciplined pursuit of virtuous actions over time molds our character, shaping us into individuals of integrity and moral strength.

3. Navigating Adversity

Discipline and consistency equip us to navigate adversity and challenges. James 1:12 (NIV) speaks of rewards for endurance: "Blessed is the one who perseveres under trial because, having stood the test, that person will receive the crown of life that the Lord has promised to those who love him." In times of difficulty, the disciplined and consistent are fortified to endure and emerge victorious.

4. Cultivating Spiritual Growth

Discipline and consistency are crucial for spiritual growth and maturity. 1 Timothy 4:7-8 (NIV) emphasizes spiritual training: "Have nothing to do with godless myths and old wives' tales; rather, train yourself to be godly. For physical training is of some value, but godliness has value for all things, holding promise for both the present life and the life to come." Consistently engaging in spiritual disciplines, such as prayer, study, and worship, fosters a deeper relationship with God.

5. Fostering Stewardship

Discipline and consistency reflect stewardship of the resources entrusted to us. Matthew 25:21 (NIV) illustrates faithfulness in stewardship: "His master replied, 'Well done, good and faithful servant! You have been faithful with a few things; I will put you in charge of many things. Come and share your master's happiness!'" The disciplined and consistent steward their time, talents, and opportunities for maximum impact.

Cultivating Discipline and Consistency

1. Clear Goals and Intentions

Discipline and consistency thrive when guided by clear goals and intentions. Proverbs 16:3 (NIV) emphasizes commitment to God: "Commit to the Lord whatever you do, and he will establish your plans." Aligning our efforts with God's purpose provides a strong foundation for disciplined and consistent action.

2. Accountability and Support

Surrounding oneself with accountability and support fosters discipline and consistency. Ecclesiastes 4:9-10 (NIV) underscores the value of partnership: "Two are better than one, because they have a good return for their labor: If either of them falls down, one can help the other up. But pity anyone who falls and has no one to help them up." Accountability partners encourage and uphold each other's commitment.

3. Overcoming Procrastination

Discipline and consistency combat procrastination, a common barrier to achievement. Proverbs 13:4 (NIV) speaks to the consequences of laziness: "A sluggard's appetite is never filled, but the desires of the diligent are fully satisfied." By overcoming procrastination through disciplined action, we realize the satisfaction of progress and accomplishment.

4. Embracing Flexibility and Adaptability

While discipline and consistency are vital, flexibility and adaptability are also important. Proverbs 19:21 (NIV) acknowledges God's ultimate plan: "Many are the plans in a person's heart, but it is the Lord's purpose that prevails." Balancing discipline with a willingness to adapt to God's leading ensures that our efforts remain aligned with His greater design.

Conclusion

The role of discipline and consistency in our lives is profound and transformative. These virtues empower us to navigate challenges, cultivate excellence, and honor God's purpose for our lives. By embracing discipline, we exercise self-control and intentional choices that shape our character and drive us toward success. By practicing consistency, we allow small, faithful actions to accumulate into meaningful outcomes, reflecting God's faithfulness in our lives.

Through the synergy of discipline and consistency, we not only achieve personal goals but also honor God in all that we do. As we draw wisdom from biblical teachings and integrate these virtues into our daily lives, we participate in a transformative journey of growth, resilience, and the fulfillment of God's purpose for our lives. Let us embrace discipline and consistency as the guiding lights that lead us to a life of purpose, impact, and unwavering devotion to our Creator.

8.2 Prioritizing self-care and stress management

Prioritizing Self-Care and Stress Management: Nurturing Well-being and Embracing God's Rest

In a world characterized by fast-paced living, demanding responsibilities, and constant connectivity, the practice of prioritizing self-care and stress management emerges as a profound way to honor God's design for our well-being. Rooted in principles of stewardship, rest, and reliance on God, this practice empowers us to cultivate a balanced and resilient life. In this exploration, we delve into the significance of self-care and stress management, drawing wisdom from biblical teachings and practical insights.

Understanding Self-Care and Stress Management

1. The Essence of Self-Care

Self-care involves intentional actions and practices that nurture physical, mental, emotional, and spiritual well-being. 1 Corinthians 6:19-20 (NIV) highlights the importance of stewardship: "Do you not know that your bodies are temples of the Holy Spirit, who is in you, whom you have received from God? You are not your own; you were bought at a price. Therefore, honor God with your bodies." Prioritizing self-care aligns with honoring God through responsible stewardship of our bodies and minds.

2. Embracing Stress Management

Stress management encompasses strategies that help us cope with and reduce the impact of stressors. Psalm 55:22 (NIV) encourages casting our burdens on God: "Cast your cares on the Lord and he will sustain you; he will never let the righteous be shaken." Effective stress management involves entrusting our worries to God while implementing practical tools to alleviate stress's effects.

Prioritizing Self-Care

1. Physical Well-being

Caring for our bodies involves proper nutrition, regular exercise, and adequate sleep. 1 Corinthians 10:31 (NIV) guides our actions: "So whether you eat or drink or whatever you do, do it all for the glory of God." Prioritizing self-care in physical health reflects our commitment to honoring God's temple.

2. Mental and Emotional Health

Nurturing mental and emotional well-being involves practices like mindfulness, relaxation, and seeking support. Philippians 4:6-7 (NIV) speaks to finding peace through prayer: "Do not be anxious about anything, but in every situation, by prayer and petition, with thanksgiving, present your requests to God. And the peace of God, which transcends all understanding, will guard your hearts and your minds in Christ Jesus." Prioritizing self-care in mental and emotional health allows us to experience the peace that surpasses understanding.

3. Spiritual Nourishment

Cultivating spiritual well-being involves prayer, meditation, scripture study, and connection with God. Psalm 1:2-3 (NIV) illustrates the benefits of delighting in God's law: "But whose delight is in the law of the Lord, and who meditates on his Law Day and night. That person is like a tree planted by streams of water, which yields its fruit in season and whose leaf does not wither—whatever they do prospers." Prioritizing self-care in spiritual growth strengthens our connection with God and anchors us in His truth.

Embracing Stress Management

1. Time Management and Boundaries

Effective time management and setting boundaries help reduce overwhelm. Psalm 90:12 (NIV) speaks to valuing time: "Teach us to number our days, that we may gain a heart of wisdom." Embracing stress management through wise time allocation and setting healthy boundaries empowers us to make the most of our days.

2. Mindfulness and Prayer

Mindfulness and prayer provide tools to manage stress by staying present and seeking divine guidance. Isaiah 26:3 (NIV) assures us of God's peace: "You will keep in perfect peace those whose minds are steadfast because they trust in you." Embracing stress management through mindfulness and prayer enables us to navigate challenges with a peaceful and grounded mindset.

3. Support and Community

Seeking support from loved ones and engaging in community fosters resilience in times of stress. Ecclesiastes 4:9-10 (NIV) underscores the value of companionship: "Two are better than one, because they have a good return for their labor: If either of them falls down, one can help the other up. But pity anyone who falls and has no one to help them up." Embracing stress management through support and community reinforces our strength and unity.

4. Rest and Sabbath Observance

Observing rest and Sabbath is a biblical principle that contributes to stress management. Exodus 20:8-10 (NIV) emphasizes Sabbath rest: "Remember the Sabbath day by keeping it holy. Six days you shall labor and do all your work, but the seventh day is a sabbath to the Lord your God." Embracing rest and observing Sabbath provides a divine rhythm that rejuvenates our spirits and aligns us with God's design for renewal.

Conclusion

Prioritizing self-care and stress management is a practice of stewardship, trust, and reliance on God's wisdom. By nurturing our physical, mental, emotional, and spiritual well-being, we honor God's design for our lives and position ourselves for growth and resilience. Embracing stress management empowers us to navigate life's challenges with grace, fortitude, and a sense of calm rooted in God's promises.

As we integrate these practices into our daily lives, we engage in a transformative journey that not only enhances our well-being but also deepens our connection with God. By prioritizing self-care and stress management, we create space for His guidance, experience His restorative power, and align ourselves with His abundant provision. Let us embrace these practices as acts of worship, recognizing that by caring for ourselves, we honor the One who lovingly crafted us and desires our wholeness.

8.3 Seeking mentorship and guidance

Seeking Mentorship and Guidance: Navigating Life's Journey with Wisdom and Godly Insight

In the tapestry of our lives, seeking mentorship and guidance emerges as a profound way to navigate the complexities of our journey. Rooted in the principles of humility, learning, and the wisdom of those who have walked before us, this practice empowers us to make informed decisions, grow spiritually, and align with God's purpose. In this exploration, we delve into the significance of seeking mentorship and guidance, drawing wisdom from biblical teachings and practical insights.

Understanding Mentorship and Guidance

1. The Essence of Mentorship

Mentorship is a relationship where a more experienced individual (the mentor) imparts wisdom, guidance, and support to someone seeking growth (the mentee). Proverbs 27:17 (NIV) illustrates the power of iron sharpening iron: "As iron sharpens iron, so one person sharpens another." Mentorship involves mutual sharpening and growth through shared experiences and wisdom.

2. The Value of Guidance

Guidance involves seeking counsel and advice from those who possess insight and understanding. Proverbs 12:15 (NIV) emphasizes the importance of seeking advice: "The way of fools seems right to them, but the wise listen to advice." Seeking guidance allows us to learn from others' perspectives and avoid pitfalls.

The Significance of Seeking Mentorship

1. Spiritual Growth

Mentorship fosters spiritual growth by providing opportunities for discipleship and learning. 2 Timothy 3:16-17 (NIV) highlights scripture's role in growth: "All Scripture is God-breathed and is useful for teaching, rebuking, correcting and training in righteousness, so that the servant of God may be thoroughly equipped for every good work." Seeking mentorship in studying scripture enables holistic spiritual development.

2. Gleaning Wisdom

Mentorship allows us to glean wisdom from those who have walked similar paths. Proverbs 13:20 (NIV) extols the value of companionship: "Walk with the wise and become wise, for a companion of fools suffers harm." Seeking mentorship enables us to tap into the wisdom that comes from shared experiences and challenges.

3. Navigating Challenges

Mentorship equips us with tools to navigate challenges and make informed decisions. Proverbs 15:22 (NIV) emphasizes the role of counsel: "Plans fail for lack of counsel, but with many advisers they succeed." Seeking mentorship helps us make well-informed choices, avoiding hasty or ill-considered actions.

4. Accountability and Encouragement

Mentorship provides accountability and encouragement on our journey. Hebrews 10:24-25 (NIV) speaks to spurring one another on: "And let us consider how we may spur one another on toward love and good deeds, not giving up meeting together, as some are in the habit of doing, but encouraging one another—and all the more as you see the Day approaching." Seeking mentorship offers a supportive network that encourages growth and perseverance.

Principles of Seeking Guidance

1. Humility

Approaching mentorship with humility allows us to receive guidance openly. Proverbs 11:2 (NIV) underscores the value of humility: "When pride comes, then comes disgrace, but with humility comes wisdom." Seeking guidance requires humility to acknowledge our limitations and learn from others.

2. Discernment

Discernment is crucial when seeking guidance to ensure alignment with biblical truths. 1 John 4:1 (NIV) exhorts us to test spirits: "Dear friends, do not believe every spirit, but test the spirits to see whether they are from God, because many false prophets have gone out into the world." Seeking mentorship involves discerning the source of advice and ensuring it aligns with God's Word.

3. Faith in God's Guidance

While seeking human mentorship, we ultimately trust in God's guidance. Proverbs 3:5-6 (NIV) speaks to trusting God's direction: "Trust in the Lord with all your heart and lean not on your own understanding; in all your ways submit to him, and he will make your paths straight." Seeking mentorship is an extension of our trust in God's ultimate plan.

Practical Steps in Seeking Mentorship

1. Identify Mentors

Identify individuals whose wisdom, character, and experiences align with your goals and values.

2. Approach with Respect

Approach potential mentors with respect and humility, expressing your desire to learn from them.

3. Communicate Goals

Clearly communicate your goals and areas in which you seek guidance and mentorship.

4. Be Teachable

Approach mentorship with a teachable spirit, open to receiving constructive feedback and advice.

5. Seek Diverse Perspectives

Seek mentorship from individuals with diverse backgrounds and perspectives to gain a well-rounded understanding.

6. Maintain Open Communication

Maintain open and regular communication with your mentor, updating them on your progress and challenges.

Conclusion

Seeking mentorship and guidance is a transformative practice that aligns us with God's wisdom, nurtures our growth, and equips us to navigate life's challenges. By humbly learning from those who have walked before us, we honor the legacy of wisdom passed down through generations. As we integrate the principles of mentorship into our lives, we recognize that seeking guidance is not a sign of weakness but a courageous step toward aligning our journey with God's purpose.

Through the guidance of mentors and the discernment rooted in biblical truths, we cultivate a life marked by growth, resilience, and a deeper understanding of God's plan. Let us embrace the wisdom of seeking mentorship, remaining teachable and open to the insights and lessons that God provides through the individuals He brings into our lives.

8.4 Surrounding yourself with positive influences

Surrounding Yourself with Positive Influences: The Science of Social Networks and Well-Being

The saying "You are the average of the five people you spend the most time with" holds more truth than one might realize. In the intricate web of human relationships, our interactions with others shape our thoughts, behaviors, and ultimately, our well-being. Scientific research has unveiled the profound impact of surrounding ourselves with positive influences on our mental, emotional, and even physical health. In this exploration, we delve into the science behind social networks and well-being, uncovering how positive influences contribute to a flourishing life.

Understanding Social Networks and Well-Being

1. The Power of Social Networks

Social networks refer to the interconnected relationships we form with family, friends, colleagues, and acquaintances. These networks play a significant role in shaping our beliefs, attitudes, and behaviors. Research published in the journal *Nature Human Behavior* (2020) highlights that social networks can influence health behaviors such as exercise, diet, and even sleep patterns.

2. Emotional Contagion

Emotional contagion refers to the phenomenon where emotions spread within social networks. A study published in the *Journal of Personality and Social Psychology* (2008) demonstrated that emotions, both positive and negative, are contagious and can be transmitted through social interactions.

The Science of Positive Influences

1. Positive Emotion Contagion

Positive emotions, such as joy, gratitude, and optimism, have been found to spread within social networks. Research published in the *Journal of Experimental Psychology: General* (2010) suggests that observing others' positive emotions can lead to an increase in one's own positive affect.

2. Neurological Mirroring

Mirror neurons in the brain play a role in empathy and imitation. Studies, including one published in *Neuron* (2010), have shown that mirror neurons contribute to the mirroring of emotions, leading to a shared emotional experience within social networks.

3. Stress Buffering

Positive social interactions have been linked to stress reduction. A study in the *Journal of Personality and Social Psychology* (2011) found that receiving support from friends and family during times of stress can lead to reduced cortisol levels and improved emotional well-being.

4. Cognitive Benefits

Engaging with positive influences can enhance cognitive functioning. A study published in the *Journal of Personality and Social Psychology* (2009) showed that exposure to positive words and images led to improved cognitive performance.

5. Longevity and Health

Positive social relationships have been associated with increased longevity and better overall health. Research published in *Social Psychological and Personality Science* (2010) found that strong social ties were linked to a 50% increased likelihood of survival over a given time period.

Practical Implications

1. Choose Your Inner Circle Wisely

Surrounding yourself with positive influences involves deliberately choosing individuals who uplift and inspire you. Research indicates that strong, positive relationships can contribute to greater life satisfaction and overall well-being.

2. Cultivate Positive Interactions

Engage in activities and interactions that promote positive emotions. Participating in group activities, volunteering, and spending time with loved ones can foster positive emotions that spread within your social network.

3. Seek Supportive Communities

Being part of supportive communities, whether in-person or online, can create a sense of belonging and provide a platform for positive interactions. Engaging with like-minded individuals who share your values can enhance your overall well-being.

4. Practice Emotional Regulation

Understanding emotional contagion underscores the importance of practicing emotional regulation. By managing your own emotions and responding positively to others' emotions, you contribute to a cycle of positive influence within your social network.

5. Nurture Reciprocal Relationships

Reciprocity is a key element of positive social interactions. By offering support, encouragement, and positivity to others, you contribute to a network of mutual benefit and well-being.

Conclusion

Scientific evidence illuminates the intricate dance between social networks and well-being. Surrounding yourself with positive influences is not just a subjective preference; it is a strategic choice that can have profound effects on your mental, emotional, and physical health. By understanding the mechanisms of emotional contagion, neurological mirroring, and stress buffering, you can harness the power of positive influences to create a ripple effect of well-being within your social circle.

As you curate your social network, remember that your choices are not only shaping your present experiences but also influencing your future outcomes. By intentionally seeking out and nurturing positive relationships, you are sowing the seeds of a more fulfilled and flourishing life. In a world where our connections are more intertwined than ever before, let the science of positive influences guide you toward a path of growth, resilience, and lasting well-being.

Surrounding Yourself with Positive Influences: Biblical Wisdom for a Fulfilling and Flourishing Life

The Bible is a timeless source of wisdom that offers profound insights into the importance of surrounding ourselves with positive influences. Throughout its pages, we find guidance on the power of relationships, the impact of community, and the significance of aligning with godly companions. Drawing from biblical principles, stories, and teachings, we explore the depth of wisdom that emphasizes the value of surrounding oneself with positive influences for a life of purpose, growth, and spiritual fulfillment.

Biblical Principles on Positive Influences

1. Proverbs 13:20 (NIV): "Walk with the wise and become wise, for a companion of fools suffers harm."

This verse highlights the importance of choosing wise companions. Surrounding oneself with wise and godly individuals leads to wisdom and spiritual growth. Just as iron sharpens iron, positive influences sharpen and refine our character and understanding.

2. Psalm 1:1-3 (NIV): "Blessed is the one who does not walk in step with the wicked or stand in the way that sinners take or sit in the company of mockers, but whose delight is in the law of the Lord, and who meditates on his Law Day and night. That person is like a tree planted by streams of water, which yields its fruit in season and whose leaf does not wither—whatever they do prospers."

This passage emphasizes the contrast between walking with the wicked and delighting in the law of the Lord. Surrounding oneself with positive influences—those who meditate on God's Word—leads to spiritual nourishment, growth, and a life that bears fruit.

3. 1 Corinthians 15:33 (NIV): "Do not be misled: 'Bad company corrupts good character."

Paul's words in this verse serve as a clear warning about the impact of negative influences. Associating with those who do not align with godly values can lead to a deterioration of our moral and spiritual character.

4. Ecclesiastes 4:9-10 (NIV): "Two are better than one, because they have a good return for their labor: If either of them falls down, one can help the other up. But pity anyone who falls and has no one to help them up."

This passage underscores the value of companionship and mutual support. Positive influences offer encouragement, accountability, and assistance in times of need, fostering a sense of unity and shared purpose.

Positive Influences in Biblical Narratives

1. The Relationship Between David and Jonathan (1 Samuel)

The friendship between David and Jonathan is a prime example of positive influence. Their mutual respect, loyalty, and encouragement to follow God's path led to David's rise to kingship and the strengthening of his faith.

2. The Gathering of Believers (Acts 2:42-47):

The early Christian community in Acts serves as a powerful model of positive influences. Their devotion to the apostles' teaching, fellowship, breaking of bread, and prayers fostered a strong sense of unity and spiritual growth.

3. Elijah and Elisha (2 Kings):

Elijah's mentoring of Elisha demonstrates the impact of positive mentorship. Elisha's desire to inherit a double portion of

Elijah's spirit reflects the aspiration to surround oneself with a godly influence for spiritual empowerment.

Practical Application of Biblical Wisdom

1. Choose Companions Wisely

Biblical wisdom encourages us to select friends and companions who share our values and are committed to spiritual growth. Surrounding ourselves with positive influences helps us stay on the path of righteousness and avoid spiritual pitfalls.

2. Seek Accountability

Being part of a community that promotes accountability and mutual encouragement strengthens our faith journey. Sharing our struggles, triumphs, and aspirations with positive influences allows us to grow together in Christ.

3. Embrace Mentoring Relationships

Just as Elisha learned from Elijah, seeking mentorship from those further along in their faith can provide valuable guidance and wisdom. Mentorship helps us navigate challenges, deepen our understanding, and align with God's purposes.

4. Contribute to Positive Environments

As followers of Christ, we are called to be positive influences ourselves. By radiating the love, grace, and truth of Jesus, we contribute to creating environments where others are inspired to grow in their faith.

Consequently, surrounding oneself with positive influences is not merely a suggestion—it is a biblical principle that echoes throughout Scripture. The wisdom of the Bible urges us to choose our companions wisely, seek accountability, embrace mentorship, and contribute to positive environments. Just as the early Christian community thrived through their devotion to God and one another, we too can experience spiritual growth, well-being, and a life of purpose by intentionally surrounding ourselves with positive influences rooted in God's Word. As we apply these principles, we honor God's design for community, nurture our faith, and contribute to a world transformed by the power of godly relationships.

CONCLUSION

Conclusion: Embracing Your Journey to Success In this final chapter, we summarize the key takeaways from the book and provide a roadmap for applying the strategies outlined. I encourage readers to embrace their unique journeys, reminding them that failure is an essential.

Embracing Your Journey to Success: Navigating Failure and Triumph

In the final chapter of this transformative journey, I have gathered the threads of wisdom woven throughout the book and offer a guiding light for applying the strategies and insights that have been explored. As you stand at the crossroads of your aspirations and dreams, it's essential to recognize that the path to success is neither linear nor free from challenges. Embracing your unique journey, failures, and triumphs is a fundamental aspect of the pursuit of success.

Summarizing the Key Takeaways

1. Fear of Failure: We've delved into the origins and impacts of the fear of failure, understanding its roots and debunking misconceptions. By shifting our mindset and cultivating self-belief, we can overcome this fear and harness its power for growth.

2. Growth Mindset: Cultivating a growth mindset involves embracing failure as a stepping stone to success. By recognizing the correlation between failure and growth, we empower ourselves to learn, adapt, and evolve.

3. Self-Compassion: Acknowledging the role of self-compassion in overcoming fear and setbacks allows us to treat ourselves with kindness and understanding. This practice fosters resilience and a deeper sense of well-being.

4. Setting Realistic Goals: The importance of setting achievable goals and breaking them down into manageable steps enables us to make consistent progress and celebrate milestones along the way.

5. Positive Mindset: Embracing positivity, gratitude, and affirmations cultivates a mental landscape that attracts success and allows us to weather challenges with resilience.

6. Mentorship and Support: Surrounding ourselves with positive influences, seeking mentorship, and engaging in supportive networks provide invaluable guidance and encouragement on our journey.

7. Self-Care and Stress Management: Prioritizing self-care, managing stress, and observing rest contribute to a balanced and thriving life.

Embracing the Journey

1. Failure as Essential: Embracing the reality that failure is an essential and inevitable part of the journey to success is a transformative perspective. Rather than shying away from failures, we can reframe them as opportunities for growth, learning, and refinement.

2. Resilience in Adversity: Embracing your journey means developing resilience in the face of adversity. Just as a tree strengthens its roots in challenging soil, setbacks can fortify your resolve and propel you forward.

3. Authenticity and Vulnerability: Embracing your journey involves embracing authenticity and vulnerability. By acknowledging your imperfections and sharing your struggles, you create connections that provide strength and support.

4. Continuous Learning: Adopting a mindset of continuous learning fuels your growth and keeps you open to new possibilities and opportunities.

5. Vision and Purpose: Craft a compelling vision for your future and align your actions with your purpose. This roadmap guides your decisions and actions, even in the face of obstacles.

6. Celebrating Small Wins: Embrace the practice of celebrating small wins along the way. Each step forward, no matter how small, is a testament to your progress and dedication.

7. Self-Belief and Perseverance: Embracing your journey requires unwavering self-belief and perseverance. Remember that success is not solely defined by the absence of failures but by your willingness to rise after each fall.

Final Thoughts

In the tapestry of your life, each chapter is interwoven with both challenges and victories. Embracing your journey is an act of courage and a declaration of faith in your ability to overcome obstacles, learn from failures, and forge a path toward your aspirations. As you step forward into the world armed with the strategies, insights, and biblical wisdom you've encountered, remember that your journey is uniquely yours. Each setback is an opportunity, each triumph a testament to your resilience.

Failure, in all its humbling and sometimes painful glory, is not a mark of defeat but a stepping stone on the path to your true potential. Embrace it, learn from it, and let it fuel your determination. The road to success is paved with moments of uncertainty, but within those moments lies the canvas upon which you paint your legacy.

So, go forth with confidence, my friend. Embrace your journey—the peaks and valleys, the triumphs and challenges—knowing that with the right mindset, the support of positive influences, and a heart aligned with purpose, you are not just pursuing success, but crafting a life of significance and impact. Embrace the journey, for within it lies the transformative power to shape not only your destiny but also the lives you touch along the way.

www.ingramcontent.com/pod-product-compliance
Lightning Source LLC
Chambersburg PA
CBHW060929140726
47996CB00001B/444